Mastering Basic S

Third Grade

Helping Children Succeed!

MW00535062

© 2006, Rainbow Bridge Publishing, Inc., Greensboro, North Carolina 27425 All rights reserved. No part of this book may be reproduced, stored in a retrieval system, or transmitted in any form or by any means (mechanically, electronically, recording, etc.) without the prior written consent of Rainbow Bridge Publishing, Inc.

ISBN 1-60022-080-0

Table of Contents

Table of Contents

Contents by Skill

Contents by Skill

Introduction

Welcome to *Mastering Basic Skills*. In third grade, children are introduced to many new and difficult skills. Third graders use comprehension skills with their reading; they are able to write a paragraph with a main idea and supporting details; they know how to use a dictionary; and they can identify the plot, setting, and main characters of a story. Third graders' math skills have also increased to include multiplication, division, and more sophisticated problem solving. Many third graders will have nightly homework and will begin to write and present simple reports.

Third grade is an academic year where children make great emotional and academic leaps. The essential skills that are being taught are more difficult. They are now reading chapter books and applying math to real-world situations. Writing is no longer done simply for practice but now has a purpose. Eager eight- and nine-year-olds are ready for these new challenges, but many have developed an "I-know-it-all" attitude and claim they are ready to take on anything that is handed their way.

Although many third graders may seem fairly confident, they still need much praise, guidance, support, and encouragement. Because they are so eager to learn (and enjoy showing off their knowledge), they sometimes will take on more than they are actually ready to handle. Children need guidance so they do not become frustrated or too self-critical when things get difficult.

Third grade children like the idea of setting goals and are able to work independently for longer periods of time. They have an understanding of choices and realize that there are consequences for making wrong choices. They are learning how to work together cooperatively and how to provide some give-and-take—these are the beginnings of the ability to compromise.

The puzzles, games, drills, and activities provided in this book will challenge children while providing them with meaningful practice. They will be able to show off their skills and have fun at the same time. That is a great combination!

Everyday Ways to Enrich Learning Experiences

Language Arts

The single most important skill that a child needs for success in school, and later in life, is to be "literate." In other words, children must learn how to read. You can do many things to encourage literacy.

- Encourage your child to read every day. Begin introducing chapter books. Have your child read a chapter a day.
- Children at this age still love to be read to. Take turns reading together.
- Ask questions. Have your child guess what is going to happen next or make up a new ending for the story.
- Go to the library and let your child choose new books.
- Write stories together. Have your child illustrate the stories.
- Have your child make a comic book.
- Fill your child's environment with literacy materials like magnetic letters, books, magazines, newspapers, catalogs, paper, pencils, crayons, paints, and CDs.
- Encourage your child to write thank-you notes or letters.
- Together make a scrapbook of third grade memories.
- Supervise your child's use of the Internet. Search for stories, games, and learning activities that your child can enjoy online. (See Web sites, page 9.)
- Take your child to a play or some type of theatrical production.
- Encourage your child to read and write poetry.
- Ask your child to look through the newspaper for information: weather, sports, local events, national news, comics, and movie listings.

Math and Science

Many toys and puzzles provide young children with early math and science learning experiences. Remember to point out all the ways we use numbers and science in our daily lives. Here are some suggested materials and activities:

- Provide blocks, puzzles, and other building materials.
- Encourage play with magnets, scales, and science books and kits.
- Have your child practice using numbers "in his head" (mental math).
- Help your child learn basic math facts. Play basic fact games.
- Play card games. This can help children learn to add quickly.
- Visit science and children's museums.
- Talk about how we use numbers in the real world: telling time, buying groceries, paying bills, and so on.
- Get your child a watch and encourage her to tell time.
- Encourage your child to begin a hobby. Encourage individual interests.
- Encourage an interest in music.

Fun Web Sites for Third Graders

http://animal.discovery.com/

This Web site for the Animal Planet cable channel is fun for animal lovers. Kids can play learning games and search the site for information on their favorite animals.

http://www.bookadventure.org/ki/index.asp

The "Book Finder" helps kids find books at a particular reading level and on specific topics chosen by the child. Some site features require free registration.

http://www.childrensmuseum.org/funonline/funonline.html

At this interactive site, kids can learn about living in space, create a multimedia project, solve science mysteries, and play online games. The Children's Museum of Indianapolis maintains this Web site.

http://funbrain.com/kidscenter.html

Site features a variety of interactive games with multiple skill levels that cover math, language arts, and science concepts.

http://www.ology.amnh.org/index.html

This interactive site will introduce kids to dinosaurs and fossils, the planets and the Milky Way, and other science topics. Kids are encouraged to collect "Ology" cards that feature fun facts, learn about the work of a paleontologist and an astronomer, read stories, solve puzzles, and play games. The site is maintained by the American Museum of Natural History in New York City.

http://www.moma.org/destination/

This site of the Museum of Modern Art in New York will take your child on a tour of the art museum. Questions guide children to look at several works of art. Children can also play games and do activities related to the works of art.

http://www.nationalgeographic.com/kids/

Site includes fun facts, coloring pages, games, homework help, and maps. Also provides a link to the online edition of National Geographic for Kids.

http://www.nga.gov/kids/kids.htm

At this Web site, visitors can watch the animated musical adventure "Lizzy and Gordon Visit the Sculpture Garden." Several pictures of paintings introduce kids to different artistic styles. The site is maintained by the National Gallery of Art.

http://sdnhm.org/kids/index.html

Kids who visit this site of the San Diego Natural History Museum can learn about dinosaur fossils and minerals and take a virtual tour about sharks living along the California coast. Games, puzzles, and activity ideas are also provided.

http://www.thunk.com

At this fun Web site, kids can change their words into secret messages for friends to unscramble. Links to FBI for Kids, CIA for Kids, and science Web sites are provided.

http://www.urbanext.uiuc.edu/conflict/index.html

At times it is not easy getting along with other people. At this Web site, kids can find out how Maria and her friends solve their problems in a peaceful way.

Recommended Books for Third Graders

A

The Adventures of Ali Baba Bernstein by
 Johanna Hurwitz
*Alexander, Who Used to Be Rich Last
 Sunday* by Judith Viorst
The Amazing Bone by William Steig
Andrew Wants a Dog by Steven Kroll
Animal Cafe by John Stadler

B

The Book of Pigericks: Pig Limericks
 by Arnold Lobel
*Brother Eagle, Sister Sky: A Message from
 Chief Seattle*, paintings by Susan Jeffers

C

*Cam Jansen and the Mystery of the
 Dinosaur Bones* by David A. Adler
*Cam Jansen and the Mystery of the
 Television Dog* by David A. Adler
Camp Ghost-Away by Judy Delton
Charlotte's Web by E. B. White
The Chinese Siamese Cat by Amy Tan
The Courage of Sarah Noble
 by Alice Dalgliesh

D

Digging Up Dinosaurs by Aliki
Dinosaur Hunters by Kate McMullan

E

The Emperor's New Clothes by Hans
 Christian Andersen

F

Fin M'Coul: The Giant of Knockmany Hill,
 retold and illustrated by Tomie de Paola
Flat Stanley by Jeff Brown
*Flatfoot Fox and the Case of the Missing
 Whoooo* by Eth Clifford
Freckle Juice by Judy Blume
Funnybones by Janet and Allan Ahlberg

G

George Washington's Breakfast
 by Jean Fritz
Girl from the Snow Country by Masako
 Hidaka
Grandfather Four Winds and Rising Moon
 by Michael Chanin
Grasshopper on the Road by Arnold Lobel

H

Harry and the Terrible Whatzit
 by Dick Gackenbach
Harry Potter books by J. K. Rowling
Helen Keller: Toward the Light by Stewart
 Graff and Polly Anne Graff
Homer Price by Robert McCloskey

I

Imogene's Antlers by David Small
In Trouble with Teacher by Patricia Brennan
 Demuth

J

*Jackie Robinson and the Story of All-Black
 Baseball* by Jim O'Connor
Just a Dream by Chris Van Allsburg
Just Plain Fancy by Patricia Polacco

K

Knots on a Counting Rope by Bill Martin, Jr.
 and John Archambault

L

The Legend of the Indian Paintbrush, retold
 and illustrated by Tomie de Paola
*The Legend of the Bluebonnet: An Old Tale
 of Texas*, retold and illustrated by Tomie
 de Paola
A Light in the Attic by Shel Silverstein
The Lorax by Dr. Seuss
Lyle, Lyle, Crocodile by Bernard Waber

M

Mag the Magnificent by Dick Gackenbach
Magic School Bus books by Joanna Cole
Making a New Home in America by
 Maxine B. Rosenberg
Maurice's Room by Paula Fox
Matreshka by Becky Hickox Ayres
The Miss Nelson books by Harry Allard and
 James Marshall
The Missing Piece Meets the Big O by Shel
 Silverstein
Miss Rumphius by Barbara Cooney
*The Monster in the Third Dresser Drawer
 and Other Stories about Adam Joshua*
 by Janice Lee Smith
Mousekin's Golden House by Edna Miller
Muggie Maggie by Beverly Cleary
*My Painted House, My Friendly Chicken,
 and Me* by Maya Angelou

N

Nate the Great books by Marjorie
 Weinman Sharmat
The New Kid on the Block: Poems
 by Jack Prelutsky
Nice New Neighbors by Franz Brandenberg
No Coins, Please by Gordon Korman
Nothing Ever Happens on My Block
 by Ellen Raskin

P

The Patchwork Quilt by Valerie Flournoy
Paul Bunyan: A Tall Tale, retold and
 illustrated by Steven Kellogg
Paul Revere by Jan Gleiter and Kathleen
 Thompson
Perfect, the Pig by Susan Jeschke
Pippi Goes on Board by Astrid Lindgren
The Polar Express by Chris Van Allsburg

R

Ramona Quimby, Age 8 by Beverly Cleary
Random House Book of Poetry for Children,
 selected and introduced by Jack
 Prelutsky
Rats on the Roof and Other Stories by
 James Marshall
The Relatives Came by Cynthia Rylant

S

*Sebastian (Super Sleuth) and the Copycat
 Crime* by Mary Blount Christian
The Spooky Tail of Prewitt Peacock
 by Bill Peet
Stone Fox by John Reynolds Gardiner
Sylvester and the Magic Pebble
 by William Steig

T

Thank You, Amelia Bedelia by Peggy Parish
Treasure Nap by Juanita Havill
*Tyrannosaurus Was a Beast: Dinosaur
 Poems* by Jack Prelutsky

U

Uncle Vova's Tree by Patricia Polacco

W

The Wild Christmas Reindeer by Jan Brett
The Wizard of Oz by L. Frank Baum
The Wump World by Bill Peet

Y

Yoo Hoo, Moon! by Mary Blocksma

Third Grade Skills Checklist

This list is an overview of some of the key skills learned in third grade. When using this list, please keep in mind that the curriculum will vary across the United States, as will how much an individual teacher is able to teach over the course of one year. The list will give you an overview of the majority of third grade skills and assist you in motivating, guiding, and helping your child maintain or even increase skills.

Language Arts/Reading

Recognizes beginning blends: bl, cl, fl, gl, pl, sl, br, cr, dr, fr, gr, pr,
 tr, sk, sm, sn, sp, st, sw, tw, scr, spl, spr, str..❑

Recognizes digraphs: ai, ay, ee, ea, oa, ue, ui, oo..❑

Recognizes r-controlled vowels: ir, ur, er, ar, or ..❑

Recognizes diphthongs: au, aw, ew, oi, ou, ow, oy...❑

Recognizes beginning digraphs: ch, sh, th, ph, qu ..❑

Recognizes ending blends: -mp, -nd, -nk, -lk, -sk, -nt, -ft, -st...........................❑

Recognizes ending digraphs: -ch, -sh, -th, -ng, -dge❑

Recognizes silent letters in consonant combinations: kn, wr, -ck, -mb, -tch❑

Recognizes compound words..❑

Recognizes contractions...❑

Recognizes antonyms, synonyms, and homonyms ..❑

Discriminates between nouns, verbs, adjectives, adverbs, and prepositions............❑

Recognizes subject and predicate ..❑

Uses plurals: -s and -es ...❑

Can divide words into syllables ..❑

Can identify the main idea of a story ..❑

Can identify the conclusion of a story ...❑

Can identify cause and effect relationships in a story ..❑

Can make predictions from context clues..❑

Draws illustrations to match sentences ..❑

Uses correct punctuation: period, question mark, exclamation point❑

Identifies types of sentences ..❑

Can use a dictionary, thesaurus, and encyclopedia ...❑

Can identify prefixes and suffixes..❑

Can write a descriptive paragraph..❑

Can write a persuasive paragraph ..❑

Is able to construct a short story ..❑

Is beginning to read and write for pleasure ..❑

Math

Recognizes odd and even numbers ..❏

Reads and writes numbers 0 to 9,999 ...❏

Understands place value to the ten thousands place❏

Knows relation and comparison symbols <, > and =❏

Can complete simple patterns ...❏

Performs two-digit addition, with regrouping ...❏

Performs two-digit subtraction, with regrouping❏

Performs three-digit addition, with regrouping ..❏

Performs three-digit subtraction, with regrouping❏

Knows multiplication facts to 9 ...❏

Knows division facts to 9 ...❏

Can multiply one-digit numbers by two-digit numbers❏

Can multiply two-digit numbers by three-digit numbers❏

Can divide one-digit numbers into two-digit numbers without remainders❏

Can divide one-digit numbers into two-digit numbers with remainders❏

Is able to solve story problems using multiplication and division❏

Can sequence events ...❏

Understands symmetry ...❏

Can write number sentences using +, −, and =❏

Can read, interpret, and create a bar graph and line graph❏

Can count money using coins in combination to $10.00❏

Can tell time in five-minute intervals ...❏

Can estimate elasped time to the hour ..❏

Understands the concept of area and perimeter....................................❏

Can measure items using standard units..❏

Can identify fractions to $\frac{1}{10}$ (unit and denominator)❏

Can add and subtract fractions with common denominators❏

Uses problem-solving strategies to complete math problems❏

Cursive Letter Practice

Trace and write the uppercase and lowercase cursive letters.

Aa Bb Cc

Dd Ee Ff

Gg Hh Ii

Jj Kk Ll

Mm Nn

Oo Pp Qq

Rr Ss Tt

Uu Vv Ww

Xx Yy Zz

Cursive Writing Evaluation

Copy the poem in your best cursive handwriting.

There was a rabbit

With a bad habit

Of jumping on places

Like crocodiles' faces!

Short and Long Vowels Review

Read each sentence. Listen to the first vowel in the highlighted word. Write ⌣ or − over the vowel and circle the correct word after the sentence.

1. Ray skied down the **slope**. long short
2. I put my picture inside a **frame**. long short
3. The **kite** was flying high in the air. long short
4. I asked Sean to **toss** the ball to me. long short
5. Ann picked a **bunch** of flowers from the field. long short
6. Tina is Marie's **sister**. long short
7. Put those papers in the **trash**. long short
8. I sat on the **bench** in the park. long short
9. The **tube** of toothpaste was empty. long short
10. Put **those** books on the shelf. long short
11. I need to get out of the sun and sit in the **shade**. long short
12. Lisa wore a white **dress** to the party. long short

Number Patterns

Study each sequence of numbers.
Circle the group of numbers that continues the pattern.

A. 1, 3, 5, 7, 9, . . .

　　　10, 11, 12, 13　　　　11, 13, 15, 17　　　　12, 14, 16, 18

B. 3, 6, 9, 12, 15, . . .

　　　18, 21, 24, 27　　　　16, 17, 18, 19　　　　30, 60, 90, 120

C. 1, 4, 7, 10, . . .

　　　12, 14, 16, 18　　　　11, 12, 13, 14　　　　13, 16, 19, 22

D. 1, 7, 13, 19, . . .

　　　21, 28, 34, 40　　　　25, 31, 37, 43　　　　21, 23, 25, 27

Ordering Numbers

Rewrite the numbers in each row in order from **least** to **greatest**.

A. 6,283 683 561 656 _____ _____ _____ _____

B. 8,899 882 8,311 411 _____ _____ _____ _____

Rewrite the numbers in each row in order from **greatest** to **least**.

C. 737 3,778 7,138 397 _____ _____ _____ _____

D. 998 899 9,989 9,998 _____ _____ _____ _____

Long and Short Vowels Assessment

Phonics

For each word, write ⌣ or – over the vowel that
correctly completes the word. Write the letter on the line.

1. wr___ck	e	u	5. tr___sh	a	e	9. r___le	u	a
2. spr___ng	u	e	6. ch___me	e	i	10. bl___ze	e	a
3. h___me	e	o	7. sc___pe	i	o	11. c___mmon	o	u
4. f___lm	a	i	8. s___ze	a	i	12. t___be	u	a

Divide a sheet of paper into two columns. Write the long vowel words from
above in one column and the short vowel words in the other column.

Addition Facts to 18

Add to solve the problems in the problem list. Then, find the same problems in the puzzle. Circle the hidden problems and write + and = in the correct places. Problems are hidden across and down.

8 + 7 = _15_	9 + 5 = ___	9 + 2 = ___	7 + 3 = ___	4 + 6 = ___
6 + 7 = ___	7 + 6 = ___	5 + 5 = ___	9 + 9 = ___	8 + 6 = ___
7 + 4 = ___	5 + 9 = ___	8 + 8 = ___	6 + 5 = ___	2 + 8 = ___
9 + 8 = ___				6 + 9 = ___
4 + 8 = ___				6 + 6 = ___

Silent e

A **silent e** at the end of a word makes the first vowel have a long sound.
Say the words and listen to the vowel sounds.

glāze thēse shīne tōte fūme

Read each word and circle the long vowel sound. Underline the silent e.

1. doze
2. brave
3. wipe
4. poke
5. thrive
6. late
7. trade

8. rise
9. tone
10. joke
11. mode
12. tile
13. twice
14. game

15. these
16. stove
17. bone
18. blame
19. side
20. kite
21. mate

Expanded Notation

Look at the key and the model for a three-digit number.
Then, fill in the missing information below.

Key

0 = hundreds
/ = tens
• = ones

Standard number: 482
Expanded notation: 400 + 80 + 2
Pictorial model: 0000 ///////// ••

A.
Standard number	Expanded notation	Pictorial model
327		

B.
Standard number	Expanded notation	Pictorial model
	200 + 50 + 4	

C.
Standard number	Expanded notation	Pictorial model
		00000000 //// •••••

Fiction or Nonfiction?

Stories can be divided into two different types. **Fiction** is drawn from the imagination, and the events and characters are not real. **Nonfiction** has only facts about people, places, subjects, and events that are real.

Read the following paragraph and write **fiction** or **nonfiction** in the box.

Army ants are some of the most feared types of ants. These ants are very destructive and can eat all living things in their paths. Army ants travel at night in groups of hundreds of thousands through the tropical forests of Africa and South America.

Now write your own story. On the bottom blank line, write whether your story is **fiction** or **nonfiction**.

Try to think of a story character you would like to be. Draw a picture of yourself as this new character.

Subtraction Facts to 18

Subtract to solve the problems in the problem lists. Then, find the same problems in the puzzle. Circle each problem and write – and = in the correct places. Problems are hidden across and down.

```
      2   8  19   0  11   4   6
      7   8   0  13  12   1   7   6  16
 11 – 5 = 6  9  16   8   1   0  12   4   9   8   1
  4  14   5   1   6   0   5   8   4   8   2   2   5  12  10
  9  19   7   3  13   6   1   0   5   4  14   7   6   7  17
 14   4   2   2   5   0  16   7   9   7  18   6   2   5  10
 10   0   6   3   0   7   8  14   3  10   1  18   9  13   5
  8   5  11   8   3  18  10   7   3   2   7  11   4   7   7
  2   3   9  14  16   6   4  12  11  19   9   8   0   9  15
  7   1   5  16   7   0  10  17   8   2  13  15   8   7  12
  9   0  11   5   7   9   6  12  15   7   8  18  14   4   9
  2   8  17   0   8  10   7   4  11   6   0   1  11   1   3
      7   5  12   2  18   9   9   6   8   9   0
      1   3   8   8   2   5   1   0   1
```

Problem List

11 – 5 = __6__

13 – 8 = _____

12 – 7 = _____

11 – 8 = _____

16 – 7 = _____

15 – 8 = _____

10 – 8 = _____

15 – 7 = _____

 5 – 0 = _____

Problem List

10 – 2 = _____

12 – 8 = _____

11 – 4 = _____

10 – 7 = _____

 4 – 2 = _____

 9 – 2 = _____

 6 – 4 = _____

18 – 9 = _____

12 – 9 = _____

Number Sentences

Read each word problem.
Circle the number sentence that shows the correct answer.

A. Brian solved two difficult math problems. It took him 11 minutes to complete the first problem and 13 minutes to complete the second. How long did it take him to complete both problems?

11 + 2 = 13 11 + 13 = 24

13 − 11 = 2 11 + 2 = 13

B. Mary invited 25 friends to her birthday party, but only 17 showed up. How many of the invited friends did not come?

17 + 25 = 43 43 − 25 = 17

25 − 17 = 8 17 − 8 = 9

C. Sharon has already read 12 pages in her science book this evening. If she has to read 18 more pages tonight, how many pages was her reading assignment for tonight?

12 + 6 = 18 18 +-12 = 30

30 + 12 = 42 18 − 6 = 12

Y as a Vowel

The letter **y** at the end of a word can make the **long e** sound or the **long i** sound.
Write each word from the word list in the correct column.

Word List

hurry
spy
fry
party
by
busy
lazy
try

1. y = $\bar{e}$ sound

2. y = $\bar{i}$ sound

Schwa Sound (ə)

Some vowels do not make a long or short sound.
These vowels make the **schwa** sound.
The symbol **ə** means a vowel makes a schwa sound.

Say the words. Listen to the schwa sound (**ə**) in each.

sofa (sofə) **lemon (lemən)** **father (fathər)**

For each pair of words, underline the schwa symbol in the first word.
Circle the vowel that makes the schwa sound in the second word.

1. systəm	s y s t e m	**2.** circəs	c i r c u s	**3.** əbout	a b o u t
4. forwərd	f o r w a r d	**5.** robən	r o b i n	**6.** aprən	a p r o n
7. chorəs	c h o r u s	**8.** camerə	c a m e r a	**9.** pencəl	p e n c i l
10. lettər	l e t t e r	**11.** ovər	o v e r	**12.** campər	c a m p e r

Story Problems

Read each word problem and circle the correct answer.
Use extra paper to help solve the problems if you need it.

A. Marcia will run every day next week. If she runs 1 mile on Sunday, 3 miles on Monday, and 5 miles on Tuesday, how many miles will she run on Wednesday?	9 7	11 13
B. John and Tonya went to the store to buy 2 boxes of oatmeal cookies. Each box has 12 cookies. How many cookies will John and Tonya have?	24 48	36 16
C. Alex has 23 marbles. If Alex has 4 friends and he gives each friend a marble, how many marbles will Alex have left?	27 4	19 20

Reading and Writing Numbers

A number is usually written using digits in the appropriate place value spots. This is called **standard form**.

Examples: five thousand, two hundred, fifty-one = **5,251**
twenty-two thousand, thirty-three = **22,033**

Write each number in standard form on the line.

A. six hundred thirty-four = _____

B. eight thousand, two hundred fifty-one = _____

C. nine thousand, three hundred twenty-two = _____

D. twenty-seven thousand, eight hundred = _____

E. seventy thousand, one hundred two = _____

F. eighty-three thousand, three hundred eleven = _____

Beginning Blends: bl, cl, fl

Write each word in the correct column.

| flute | blue | clean | clasp | float | fleet | blimp | blink | cloak |

bl	cl	fl
_____	_____	_____
_____	_____	_____
_____	_____	_____

Expanded Notation

Expanded notation is writing a number to show the value of each digit in the number. **Examples:** 583 = **500 + 80 + 3**

six hundred fifty-two = **600 + 50 + 2**

Circle the letter beside the correct expanded notation for each number.

Eight hundred seventy-five =

A. 8,000 + 70 + 5

B. 800 + 70 + 5

C. 80,000 + 700 + 50

D. 800,000 + 70 + 5

Six thousand forty-eight =

A. 6,000 + 400 + 80

B. 10,000 + 6,000 + 400 + 80

C. 6,000 + 40 + 8

D. 60,000 + 40 + 8

Beginning Blends: gl, pl, sl

Say the word that names each picture.
Circle the beginning blend of each word.

1.

gl
pl
sl

2.

gl
pl
sl

3.

gl
pl
sl

4.

gl
pl
sl

5.

gl
pl
sl

6.

gl
pl
sl

Nouns

Common nouns name any one of a group of things.
Proper nouns name a specific person, place, or thing.

Each sentence has one common noun and one proper noun. Write the common noun to the left of the sentence and the proper noun to the right.

Common Nouns

 My cousin lives in Spain.

Smokey is a famous bear.

My family ate at Pizza Barn.

Ogden is a beautiful city.

Isaac Newton was a scientist.

The first satellite was Sputnik I.

George Eastman made cameras.

The Pilgrims sailed for two months.

Proper Nouns

Comparing Numbers

Study the examples below. To compare each pair of numbers, use less than (‹), greater than (›), or equal to (=). Write the correct symbol in each oval.

Examples: 375 (‹) 6,200 7,000 (=) 7,000 3,482 (›) 2,843

A. 620 ◯ 6,200

B. 493 ◯ 439

C. 6,432 ◯ 16,408

D. 9,286 ◯ 13,489

E. 724 ◯ 724

F. 3,080 ◯ 3,800

G. 45,015 ◯ 45,016

H. 397,124 ◯ 387,425

I. 488,188 ◯ 488,018

Two-Digit Addition with Regrouping

Add to solve the problems.

A. 54
 +26

B. 44
 +39

C. 19
 +76

D. 24
 +47

E. 38
 +57

F. 29
 +64

G. 49
 +31

H. 78
 +12

I. 36
 +46

Beginning Blends: br, cr, dr, fr

Say the name of each picture. Fill in the circle if
the word begins with the blend in the box.

1.
dr

○

2.
cr

○

3.
br

○

4.
fr

○

5.
cr

○

6.
br

○

7.
cr
○

8.
br
○

9.
fr

○

10.
dr

○

11.
fr

○

12.
dr

○

27

Beginning Blends: gr, pr, tr

Say the names of the pictures.
Circle the picture that begins with each blend shown.

1.
gr

2.
pr

3.
tr

Read each word. Circle the beginning blend **gr**, **pr**, or **tr** in each word.

4. preview	5. produce	6. truly	7. triumph
8. tread	9. prop	10. tree	11. predict
12. grew	13. ground	14. gruel	15. grant

Two-Digit Subtraction with Regrouping

Subtract to solve the problems.

A.
70
−19

B.
82
−17

C.
70
−22

D.
90
−79

E.
78
−59

F.
53
−14

G.
66
− 8

H.
54
−38

Pronouns

Circle the **pronoun** that completes each sentence.

1. _____ grew corn and tomatoes in his garden.

 Him His He

2. Please tell _____ what vegetables you would like to plant this year.

 we mine us

3. Tisha and _____ love to plant our watermelon seeds.

 we I us

4. Mother wants to plant flowers in her garden so that _____ will have something special.

 us mine she

5. We plant carrots, lettuce, and beans because _____ are good to eat.

 they them she

Addition with Regrouping

A.
$$35 + 27$$

B.
$$85 + 56$$

C.
$$28 + 14$$

D.
$$78 + 66$$

E.
$$348 + 235$$

F.
$$628 + 597$$

G.
$$565 + 217$$

H.
$$4,188 + 176$$

Adding Two or More Addends

Keep the place values lined up to find the right sum. Solve the problems.

A. 62
 + 27

B. 75
 + 85

C. 54
 + 92

D. 736
 89
 + 104

E. 3,482
 437
 + 68

F. 246
 442
 + 53

G. 6,428
 1,375
 + 3,684

H. 30,147
 25,236
 + 42,613

I. 2,804
 1,366
 + 5,391

J. 5,894
 1,388
 + 3,137

K. 28,123
 33,294
 + 46,510

L. 14,738
 22,856
 + 17,979

Beginning Blends: sk, sm, sn, sp

Say the name of each picture. Circle the word that names the picture and write its beginning blend.

1.

smell
spoon
skill

2.

smoke
spy
snack

3.

skunk
snowman
snare

4.

smear
spore
skate

5.

smack
skirt
sniff

6.

spool
skit
snoop

7.

smile
sneak
spoof

8.

skull
spill
snail

Action Verbs

An **action verb** tells what the subject of a sentence does.
Look at the action verbs in the following sentences.
Dino plays football in the fall. **We walk home every day.**

Underline the **action verb** in each sentence.

1. Small airplanes fly over our house every afternoon at 5:00.

2. The rooster on our farm crows every morning at 6:00.

3. My dad plows the fields near our house in the spring.

4. The ducks in the pond splash water everywhere each afternoon.

5. Mother feeds the chickens twice a day.

6. My brother and I clean the barn every Saturday.

Two-Digit Subtraction

Math

Subtract to solve the problems.

A. 17 − 16	**B.** 46 − 25	**C.** 84 − 53	**D.** 78 − 16
E. 25 − 14	**F.** 27 − 13	**G.** 75 − 31	**H.** 68 − 14
I. 23 − 12	**J.** 42 − 31	**K.** 24 − 13	**L.** 82 − 71

Large Number Subtraction

Solve the problems.

A.	B.	C.	D.
52 −39	47 −19	61 −25	980 −430
E. 543 −298	F. 766 −384	G. 7,303 −3,855	H. 8,624 −4,937
I. 5,322 −1,404	J. 49,718 −32,579	K. 38,972 −24,687	L. 15,476 −13,287

Correct Spellings

Look at the words in each row. Circle the **correctly spelled** word.

1. buzes — buzzes — buzzis
2. schol — schoul — school
3. sumtim — sometime — sometme
4. baloon — balloon — ballon
5. work — wrok — werk
6. monoy — money — monie
7. chaneg — chang — change
8. reding — raeding — reading
9. homework — homwork — homewrok

Multiplication Tables for Basic Facts 0-9

Glue these tables onto index cards and use them to practice your facts.

0

0 x 0 = 0	0 x 5 = 0
0 x 1 = 0	0 x 6 = 0
0 x 2 = 0	0 x 7 = 0
0 x 3 = 0	0 x 8 = 0
0 x 4 = 0	0 x 9 = 0

5

5 x 0 = 0	5 x 5 = 25
5 x 1 = 5	5 x 6 = 30
5 x 2 = 10	5 x 7 = 35
5 x 3 = 15	5 x 8 = 40
5 x 4 = 20	5 x 9 = 45

1

1 x 0 = 0	1 x 5 = 5
1 x 1 = 1	1 x 6 = 6
1 x 2 = 2	1 x 7 = 7
1 x 3 = 3	1 x 8 = 8
1 x 4 = 4	1 x 9 = 9

6

6 x 0 = 0	6 x 5 = 30
6 x 1 = 6	6 x 6 = 36
6 x 2 = 12	6 x 7 = 42
6 x 3 = 18	6 x 8 = 48
6 x 4 = 24	6 x 9 = 54

2

2 x 0 = 0	2 x 5 = 10
2 x 1 = 2	2 x 6 = 12
2 x 2 = 4	2 x 7 = 14
2 x 3 = 6	2 x 8 = 16
2 x 4 = 8	2 x 9 = 18

7

7 x 0 = 0	7 x 5 = 35
7 x 1 = 7	7 x 6 = 42
7 x 2 = 14	7 x 7 = 49
7 x 3 = 21	7 x 8 = 56
7 x 4 = 28	7 x 9 = 63

3

3 x 0 = 0	3 x 5 = 15
3 x 1 = 3	3 x 6 = 18
3 x 2 = 6	3 x 7 = 21
3 x 3 = 9	3 x 8 = 24
3 x 4 = 12	3 x 9 = 27

8

8 x 0 = 0	8 x 5 = 40
8 x 1 = 8	8 x 6 = 48
8 x 2 = 16	8 x 7 = 56
8 x 3 = 24	8 x 8 = 64
8 x 4 = 32	8 x 9 = 72

4

4 x 0 = 0	4 x 5 = 20
4 x 1 = 4	4 x 6 = 24
4 x 2 = 8	4 x 7 = 28
4 x 3 = 12	4 x 8 = 32
4 x 4 = 16	4 x 9 = 36

9

9 x 0 = 0	9 x 5 = 45
9 x 1 = 9	9 x 6 = 54
9 x 2 = 18	9 x 7 = 63
9 x 3 = 27	9 x 8 = 72
9 x 4 = 36	9 x 9 = 81

Syllables

Answer the questions. Write the answers on the lines.

newt

hip•po•pot•a•mus

star•fish

en•cy•clo•pe•di•a

ta•ran•tu•la

1. Which word has five syllables? _____

2. How many syllables does **encyclopedia** have? _____

3. Which word has three syllables? _____

4. How many syllables does **starfish** have? _____

5. Which word has one syllable? _____

6. How many syllables does **tarantula** have? _____

zuc•chi•ni

Multiplication Facts for 0

Math

When the number **0** is a factor, the product is always **0**.

$$3 \times 0 = 0 \qquad 0 \times 9 = 0$$

Complete the facts for 0.

0 × 0 = ___ 0 × 5 = ___

0 × 1 = ___ 0 × 6 = ___

0 × 2 = ___ 0 × 7 = ___

0 × 3 = ___ 0 × 8 = ___

0 × 4 = ___ 0 × 9 = ___

Pictograph

The following **pictograph** shows the favorite pets of students in Mrs. Mill's third grade class. Each picture stands for one student's vote.

Favorite Pets

Number of Votes

Iguanas Snakes Gerbils Cats Dogs

Look at the graph and answer the questions.

A. How many children voted for gerbils? _____

B. What pet received the fewest votes? _____

C. How many more votes did cats receive than snakes? _____

D. How many children voted in all? _____

E. Which two pets were equally popular? _____

Multiplication Facts for 1

When the number **1** is a factor, the product equals the other factor.

$$1 \times 9 = 9 \qquad 2 \times 1 = 2$$

Complete the facts for 1.

$1 \times 0 = \underline{\quad}$ $1 \times 5 = \underline{\quad}$

$1 \times 1 = \underline{\quad}$ $1 \times 6 = \underline{\quad}$

$1 \times 2 = \underline{\quad}$ $1 \times 7 = \underline{\quad}$

$1 \times 3 = \underline{\quad}$ $1 \times 8 = \underline{\quad}$

$1 \times 4 = \underline{\quad}$ $1 \times 9 = \underline{\quad}$

Beginning Blends: st, sw, tw

Say each word below. If the word begins with the **st** blend, circle it.
If the word begins with the **sw** blend, draw an **X** on it.
If the word begins with the **tw** blend, underline it.

1. twelve 2. staple 3. twist 4. tweak 5. swan 6. stand

7. swat 8. swipe 9. sting 10. sweep 11. twilight 12. stare

Say the name of each picture. Write the two letters that
make up the word's beginning blend.

13. **14.** **15.** **16.** **17.** **18.**

Beginning Blends: scr, spl, spr, str

Circle the **beginning blend** in each word below.

1. scratch 2. stride 3. sprinkle 4. spruce 5. splay
6. sprig 7. split 8. scribble 9. straight 10. street
11. splurge 12. scroll 13. stream 14. spray 15. sprig

Use the beginning blend **scr**, **spl**, **spr**, or **str**
to complete the name of each picture.

16. _____ ub

17. _____ inter

18. _____ ing

19. _____ eam

20. _____ oller

21. _____ inkler

Multiplication Facts for 2

Multiply to solve the problems.

A. 3
 x 2

B. 8
 x 2

C. 0
 x 2

D. 2
 x 6

E. 2
 x 5

F. 2
 x 7

G. 4
 x 2

H. 2
 x 2

I. 2
 x 9

J. 1
 x 2

K. 2
 x 8

L. 2
 x 5

Story Webs

Complete the story web. Use the words in the web to write a story. Be sure to use capital letters and periods. Think of a title for your story.

Things to Think About

Who is this story about?

Where does this story take place?

How does this story begin?

What happens next?

How will this story end?

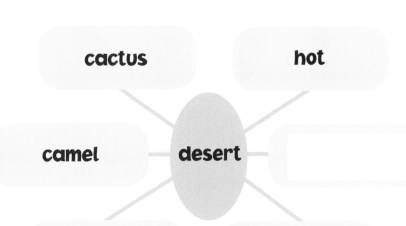

Multiplication Facts for 3

Use the sets below to help complete the multiplication facts.

A. 1 x 3 = _____ **B.** 9 x 3 = _____ **C.** 4 x 3 = _____

D. 5 x 3 = _____ **E.** 6 x 3 = _____ **F.** 2 x 3 = _____

G. 3 x 3 = _____ **H.** 7 x 3 = _____ **I.** 8 x 3 = _____

J. 0 x 3 = _____ **K.** 3 x 9 = _____ **L.** 3 x 3 = _____

Vowel Sound ai/ay

Write a word from the word list under each picture.

Word List waist ray crayon paint hay train

1.

2.

3.

4.

5.

6.

Word SearcheS

1

Parties!

Circle the words from the word list in the puzzle below.

Word List

party
celebrate
birthday
decorate
special
excited
surprise
invite
ribbon
balloon

```
I C R I B B O N T E
N E B L E S Y A M X
A L S I N V I T E C
D E C O R A T E U I
E B J E F T G R M T
C R C S U R H E A E
B A L L O O N D H D
I T N S P E C I A L
R E X C I P A R T Y
T R S U R P R I S E
```

3

Circle the words from the word list in the puzzle below.

```
B A R E M T A D H S
L W A D M I R E S T
D A C H I E V E P U
S R B L O A C D O D
P D I R S C F M T E
E U Q B U T L I L N
C T X S B A S R I T
I S H I K O D A G S
A D O W B S N X H C
L P R E F F O R T M
```

2

Word List

award
effort
ribbon
students
achieve
success
special
admire
spotlight
deed

Circle the words from the word list in the puzzle below.

```
F D R O M A S C O T
I S A U N I F O R M
A C P S D G U M F A
L H E O T E M P E L
D A H P R S H E M G
W M S L N T R T U D
H P G A M E S E L X
U I D Y F J H E O K
Y O V E R T I M E H
S N R R E F U N A P
```

4

Word List

sports
compete
field
referee
game
player
uniform
mascot
champion
overtime

Bath Time

Circle the words from the word list in the puzzle below.

Word List

bathtub
bubbles
soap
clean
water
lather
splash
towel
scrub
washcloth

```
S  J  D  R  E  K  E  L  O  R
I  P  H  S  G  C  W  P  N  X
B  C  L  E  A  N  A  R  P  Y
K  A  A  P  O  C  H  V  O
W  S  T  O  S  W  A  T  E  R
N  C  H  H  K  H  G  O  S  F
C  R  E  I  T  R  A  W  T  E
P  U  R  P  V  U  V  E  U  N
S  B  E  B  U  B  B  L  E  S
D  W  A  S  H  C  L  O  T  H
```

5

Air Travel

Circle the words from the word list in the puzzle below.

Word List

airplane
pilot
baggage
cabin
ticket
landing
depart
flight
hangar
tower

```
M  E  T  I  C  K  E  T  I  H
N  O  W  A  N  D  R  L  W  D
F  L  I  G  H  T  F  I  R  E
E  A  B  V  T  A  K  B  N  P
L  N  R  U  O  J  N  A  E  A
P  D  I  T  W  U  L  G  E  R
F  I  R  H  E  P  R  G  A  T
A  N  K  S  R  D  N  A  R  R
W  G  P  I  L  O  T  G  W  E
T  C  A  B  I  N  S  E  L  V
```

7

43

Farming

Circle the words from the word list in the puzzle below.

```
L J U T N E P M J S
I S H O R S E S F O
V B I B X A S D E Q
E H A L U P C I R U
S A W R O O S T E R
T R E R N G N B O K
O V C A H Y C T H R
C E V X S T A B L E
K S F A R M E R P W
G T N E Y D R A D S
```

6

Word List

farmer
tractor
crops
rooster
horses
stable
barnyard
livestock
harvest
silo

Bicycles

Circle the words from the word list in the puzzle below.

```
W H E A C I W P N O
P K P E D K H A E P
B I C Y C L E R D A
R C B O R S E A T T
I K L F P I L P E H
E S O P A J D M A T
D T L E T S L E X K
H A N D L E B A R B
S N K A H C H A I N
E D B L T R P O G L
```

8

Word List

bicycle
seat
rider
chain
wheel
path
handlebar
pedal
kickstand
park
helmet
lock

Punctuation Marks

Each sentence below is missing a punctuation mark.
Put the correct **punctuation mark** in each place that needs one.

1. Mario had a hamburger, some potatoes, and a milk shake for dinner. He can t eat another bite!

2. Mr. and Mrs Blair went to the movies last night with their three children.

3. Did you know that Maple Ave. crosses Second St at Main?

4. Dr. Barnes was able to see Mark yesterday afternoon

5. José and Latasha visited Maine, Vermont New York, and New Hampshire this past summer.

6. Is New York abbreviated NJ, NC, or NY

7. Don hit two home runs in the game. His team won

8. Wow What a neat costume! I wish I were a pirate!

9. Benita thinks that she would like to be a doctor but she also thinks that she may become a teacher.

10. Bernie s favorite ice-cream flavors are chocolate, vanilla, butter pecan, and maple nut.

Vowel Sound ee/ea

Complete each word by writing the letters **ee** or **ea** on the line.

1. wh _____ l
2. ind _____ d
3. cl _____ n
4. l _____ ve
5. sp _____ k
6. sn _____ ze
7. tr _____ t
8. sl _____ p
9. s _____ n
10. b _____ p
11. sl _____ t
12. tr _____
13. dr _____ m
14. str _____ t
15. gr _____ se

BONUS

Write **ee** or **ea** to make each word match the clue.

st _____ l
(hard metal)

p _____ k
(to look)

w _____ k
(not strong)

Multiplication Facts for 4

When a number is multiplied by 4, it is the same as adding the number to itself 4 times.

$4 \times 3 = 12$ is the same as $3 + 3 + 3 + 3 = 12$

Complete the facts for 4.

$4 \times 0 =$ _____ $4 \times 5 =$ _____

$4 \times 1 =$ _____ $4 \times 6 =$ _____

$4 \times 2 =$ _____ $4 \times 7 =$ _____

$4 \times 3 =$ _____ $4 \times 8 =$ _____

$4 \times 4 =$ _____ $4 \times 9 =$ _____

Multiplication Facts for 5

Use the sets of 5 below to help complete the multiplication facts.

A. $4 \times 5 =$ ____

B. $4 \times 5 =$ ____

C. $8 \times 5 =$ ____

D. $7 \times 5 =$ ____

E. $2 \times 5 =$ ____

F. $9 \times 5 =$ ____

G. $3 \times 5 =$ ____

H. $6 \times 5 =$ ____

I. $1 \times 5 =$ ____

Vowel Sound oa

Use the words from the word list to complete each sentence.
Circle the **long o** sound of **oa** in each word.

Word List

loan
afloat
coach
oak
toaster
coast

1. Mr. Collins is our basketball _____.
2. The acorns fell from the _____ tree.
3. We hoped our raft would stay _____ in the water.
4. The storm hit the Florida _____ last night.
5. Mindy asked if I would _____ her my bike.
6. Put the bread in the _____, then butter it.

Complete each word by writing the letters **oa**. Read the word and listen for the **long o** sound.

7. r____d
8. c____l
9. t____d
10. g____t
11. l____d
12. b____t
13. s____p
14. g____l
15. ____ts

47

Vowel Sound ue/ui

Complete each word by writing **ue** or **ui** on the line.
Read the words and listen for the **long u** sound.

1. s_____t

2. cr_____l

3. s_____

4. fr_____t

5. br_____se

6. f_____l

7. tr_____

8. d_____

9. d_____l

10. n_____sance

11. cr_____se

12. j_____ce

13. cl_____

14. gl_____

15. T_____sday

Logical Thinking

Read the following word problems. Make notes to help you find the
order of the people in each problem. Circle the correct answer.

A. Four marathon runners ran in a race. Use the clues to determine the winner.

Mario ran faster than Shane.

Shane ran faster than Randy.

Tyler ran faster than Mario.

Who won the race?

 a. Mario c. Shane

 b. Randy d. Tyler

B. Davis lined up his four sisters by height. Use the clues below to determine the order of the sisters.

Sally is taller than Kendra.

Mary is the tallest sister.

Trisha is not as tall as Kendra.

In what order did the sisters stand?

a. Mary, Trisha, Kendra, Sally
b. Mary, Sally, Trisha, Kendra
c. Mary, Sally, Kendra, Trisha
d. Sally, Mary, Trisha, Kendra

Main Idea

A paragraph is a group of detail sentences that support a **main idea**.
The main idea is usually in the topic sentence at the beginning
of the paragraph.

Look at each paragraph below and circle the main idea.
Underline the detail sentence that does **not** support the main idea.

1. Yesterday my class visited the zoo. We were amazed at all the animals that lived there. There were animals from all over the world in their natural habitats. I live in a house. My favorite animal was the elephant who lived on the African plains.

2. We played a game in our classroom yesterday called Silent Ball. To play this game everyone must stand in a circle and be absolutely silent. A sponge ball is then passed from person to person. The ball may be passed to a person next to you or to a person across the room. Mary does not like the game, so she chose not to play. If a player misses the ball or makes a sound, he must sit down. The last person standing is the winner of this soundless game.

3. José has an unusual pet. It is an iguana named Pete. Pete lives in a glass house made from an old fish aquarium. He eats a special diet of fruit and green plants. Sleeping at night and being active during the day is Pete's normal routine. My friend Martin has an iguana at his house, too. Pete has a greenish gray appearance and blends into his environment. Jose's unusual pet is fun to observe.

Beat the Clock (Multiplication Facts to 5)

A.
4×3 3×1 2×2 5×5 3×5 0×3 4×2 1×4 2×0 5×2

B.
5×5 4×2 0×5 4×4 1×5 2×3 5×4 2×5 0×1 3×3

C.
0×2 3×1 5×1 4×5 3×0 1×1 2×2 0×1 4×0 1×2

D.
2×3 3×4 2×0 5×3 2×5 4×4 0×0 3×1 5×2 1×2

E.
5×0 1×3 2×1 3×2 0×2 4×1 3×4 1×0 3×5 5×1

F.
2×4 0×5 0×0 4×2 3×3 1×5 1×1 4×1 3×0 0×4

G.
5×4 2×1 0×0 1×5 5×0 4×4 1×2 2×5 5×1 2×4

H.
4×0 5×2 1×4 3×0 3×2 1×3 5×3 0×1 2×2 4×3

I.
4×5 0×3 3×2 4×3 1×1 2×3 3×5 2×1 1×4 5×5

J.
3×4 1×0 5×4 4×1 5×3 0×4 4×5 1×3 2×4 3×3

Time: _____ **Number correct:** _____

Compare and Contrast

Fill in the blanks with words that tell how a cat and dog are alike and different. The first ones have been done for you.

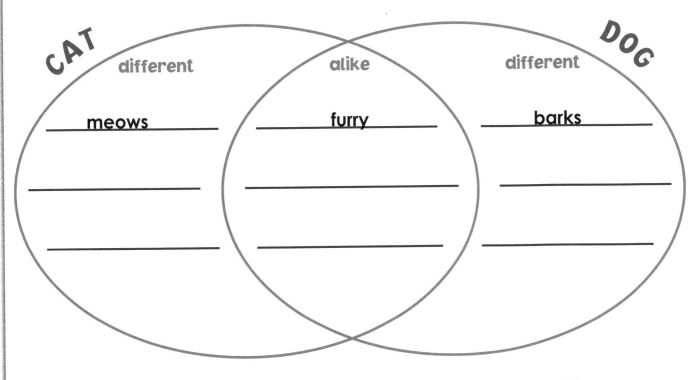

CAT

DOG

different

alike

different

meows

furry

barks

Write two paragraphs below. In the first paragraph, tell how cats and dogs are alike. Tell how each is different in the second paragraph. Give each paragraph a title.

_____ _____

_____ _____

_____ _____

_____ _____

_____ _____

_____ _____

Fractions

Fractions show parts of the whole.

Circle the correct fraction to answer each question.

A. What part of the drawing is shaded?

$\frac{2}{5}$ $\frac{1}{4}$ $\frac{4}{5}$ $\frac{2}{3}$

B. What part of the drawing is shaded?

$\frac{1}{3}$ $\frac{1}{4}$ $\frac{3}{4}$ $\frac{2}{4}$

C. Which fraction names the shaded part of the set?

$\frac{3}{4}$ $\frac{1}{2}$ $\frac{2}{3}$ $\frac{5}{6}$

D. Which fraction names the shaded part of the set?

$\frac{1}{2}$ $\frac{3}{4}$ $\frac{2}{3}$ $\frac{1}{3}$

Vowel Digraph oo

Compare the sound of the letters **oo** in the words **look** and **moon**.
Read each word and circle the matching sound.

ŏŏ = look ōō = moon

1. gloomy ŏŏ ōō 2. spooky ŏŏ ōō 3. crook ŏŏ ōō

4. boot ŏŏ ōō 5. proof ŏŏ ōō 6. rooster ŏŏ ōō

7. book ŏŏ ōō 8. foolish ŏŏ ōō 9. cook ŏŏ ōō

10. wool ŏŏ ōō 11. scoop ŏŏ ōō 12. took ŏŏ ōō

13. stood ŏŏ ōō 14. broom ŏŏ ōō 15. cookie ŏŏ ōō

Identifying and Using Polygons

Circle the correct answer for each question.

A. Which figure has four sides?

B. Which figure is a triangle?

C. What shape is the top surface of a can of soup?

triangle square

circle rectangle

D. Which figure can Roberto build using exactly seven squares?

R-Controlled Sounds: ar, or

Read each sentence. Write the correct word to complete the sentence. Circle the r-controlled vowel.

1. Sam is a good _____, so he shook hands with Mike after the game. (sport spart)

2. Our plane will _____ from the airport at 2:00.
(depart deport)

3. Our class will _____ a song in the spring concert.
(perform perfarm)

4. My brother and I are taking _____ lessons.
(guitor guitar)

5. Ann walks her dog each _____ and afternoon.
(morning marning)

6. Rachel is my _____ in the science project.
(partner portner)

Symmetry

Symmetry occurs when two halves of a figure match exactly when folded together. The line of symmetry is the location of the fold.

Example: This square shows a **line of symmetry** from top to bottom (vertical).

In each group, circle the figure that has a line of symmetry.

A. **B.** **C.**

R-Controlled Sounds: er, ir, ur

Choose a word from the word list to complete each sentence.
Circle the letters that make the r-controlled vowel sound.

1. Please _____ the room quietly.

2. I put the money in my mother's _____.

3. Sally won the _____ place ribbon in the race.

4. The _____ took my temperature.

5. We went to the movies _____ lunch.

6. The ballerina loved to _____.

Word List

first
enter
after
nurse
twirl
purse

Circle the letters that make the r-controlled vowel sound in each word.

7. p e r f e c t 8. c u r b 9. r u b b e r 10. n u r s e

11. b r o t h e r 12. u r g e 13. h e r m i t 14. t u r t l e

15. w h i r l 16. p u r s e 17. c u r t a i n 18. p u r p l e

Multiplication Facts 0-5

Multiply to solve the problems in the problem list.
Then, find the same problems in the puzzle. Circle the
hidden problems and write **x** and **=** in the correct places.
Problems are hidden across and down.

Problem List

1 x 4 = __4__
5 x 3 = _____
3 x 4 = _____
0 x 3 = _____
4 x 4 = _____
2 x 4 = _____
1 x 2 = _____
5 x 5 = _____
3 x 3 = _____
0 x 1 = _____
4 x 5 = _____
2 x 2 = _____
1 x 1 = _____
5 x 2 = _____
3 x 2 = _____
4 x 2 = _____
4 x 1 = _____
2 x 1 = _____
4 x 3 = _____

Puzzle grid:

1	5	0	4	2	0	2	6
2	4	8	3	3	4	5	20
20	0	1	12	7	16	2	0
0	3	0	1	12	0	3	1
2	6	1	2	9	1	7	4
1	5	5	25	5	0	4	8
2	12	3	3	9	8	4	12
1 x 4 = 4	6	1	2	16	7		
7	3	4	12	1	3	10	5
4	0	25	7	1	20	1	3
2	18	3	3	2	2	4	15
8	6	1	16	0	5	2	10
24	8	2	8	3	2	6	15
0	10	2	4	1	4	15	9

New Vocabulary Words

Use a dictionary to help you answer the questions below.
You will have fun learning some new words and interesting facts.
Look up the highlighted words and answer the questions on the lines.

1. Is a **goldfinch** a bag full of gold or a bird?

2. If you were on a **jetty**, would you be on a jet or a wall along
 a waterfront?

3. Is a **yak** a long-haired ox or a person that likes to talk?

4. Would you draw a **parallelogram** or do gymnastics on it?

Math

Multiplication Facts for 6

When a number is multiplied by 6, it is the
same as adding the number to itself 6 times.

$6 \times 3 = 18$ is the same as $3 + 3 + 3 + 3 + 3 + 3 = 18$

Complete the facts for 6.

$6 \times 0 =$ ___ $6 \times 5 =$ ___

$6 \times 1 =$ ___ $6 \times 6 =$ ___

$6 \times 2 =$ ___ $6 \times 7 =$ ___

$6 \times 3 =$ ___ $6 \times 8 =$ ___

$6 \times 4 =$ ___ $6 \times 9 =$ ___

Understanding What I Read

Read the story. Then, answer the questions.

The Wright Brothers

Orville and Wilbur Wright were famous American brothers. They owned a bicycle shop in Dayton, Ohio. Although they were interested in bicycles, they also loved the idea of flying. In 1896, they began to experiment, or try new ideas, with flight. They started by testing kites and then gliders, which are motorless planes. These tests taught them how an airplane should rise, turn, and come back to earth. The brothers made over 700 glider flights at Kitty Hawk, in North Carolina. This was fun but not good enough for them. Orville and Wilbur put a small engine on a plane they named *Flyer I*. On December 17, 1903, they took the first motor-powered flight that lasted about one minute. The brothers continued to experiment until they could stay in the air for over one hour.

1. What was the main idea of the story? Circle the correct answer.
 a. Testing new ideas is important.
 b. *Flyer I* was the first airplane.
 c. The Wright brothers were early pilots.

2. What does the word **experiment** mean? Circle the correct answer.
 a. to try new ideas
 b. to test kites
 c. to stay in the air for one hour

3. Where did the brothers test their gliders and plane? _____

4. How long did their first motor-powered flight last? _____

5. How did the brothers learn about what makes planes work? _____

Diphthong au

Complete each sentence with a word from the word list.
Write the word and circle the **au** diphthong.

Word List

applause	vault	naughty
because	fault	caught

1. The _____ was coming from the theater.

2. The bank teller got money from the _____.

3. We _____ 10 fish on our fishing trip.

4. It was my _____ that we were late for the movie.

5. The _____ puppy chewed up the shoe.

6. We did not have school yesterday _____ it was a holiday.

Multiplication Facts for 7

Multiply to solve the problems.

A. 3
 x 7

B. 1
 x 7

C. 7
 x 7

D. 8 x 7 = _____

E. 7 x 9 = _____

F. 2 x 7 = _____

G. 7
 x 6

H. 7
 x 4

I. 7
 x 5

J. 4 x 7 = _____

K. 7 x 3 = _____

L. 9 x 7 = _____

Multiplication Facts for 8

Multiply to solve the problems.

A. 4
 x 8

B. 8
 x 8

C. 6
 x 8

D. 7 x 8 = _____

E. 3 x 8 = _____

F. 5 x 8 = _____

G. 8
 x 0

H. 8
 x 1

I. 9
 x 8

Diphthong aw

Read each sentence. Write the correct word to complete the sentence.

1. We cut down the tree with a _____.
 (saw sau)

2. The farmer put _____ in the barn to keep the horses warm.
 (straw strau)

3. We stood under the _____ so we would not get wet.
 (awning auning)

4. The little _____ could hardly walk.
 (faun fawn)

5. Put the meat on the counter to _____.
 (thaw thau)

6. We gazed in _____ as the acrobat walked on the high wire.
 (aue awe)

7. My baby brother will _____ before he learns to walk.
 (craul crawl)

Grid Coordinates

Look at the lines on the grid below. **Grid coordinates** are formed by the letters on the bottom and the numbers on the left side. If you look at the coordinates (C, 4), you should find the Enchanted Woods.

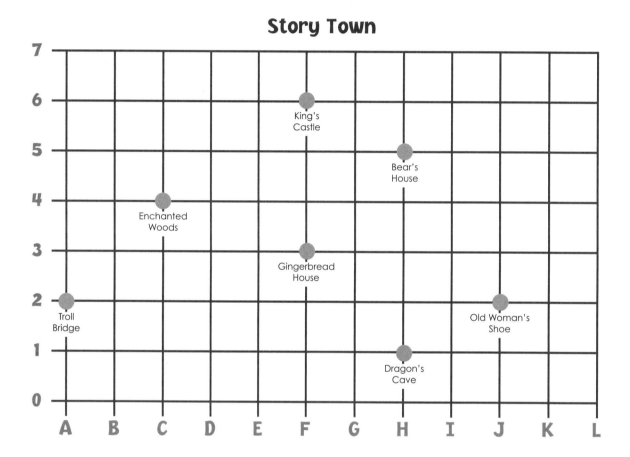

Look at each fairy-tale place on the map and find its coordinates.
Write the coordinates for each place beside its name.

King's Castle _____, _____ Gingerbread House _____, _____

Troll Bridge _____, _____ Dragon's Cave _____, _____

Bear's House _____, _____ Old Woman's Shoe _____, _____

Poetry—Haiku

Haiku is a form of Japanese poetry that follows a special pattern of 17 syllables. There are 5 syllables in the first line, 7 in the second line, and 5 in the third line. Most haiku poetry is about nature.

Read the following haiku poem.

Flakes of snow outside.

Icicles hanging from eaves.

Winter is here now.

Use the lines to write a Haiku poem of your own about apples, summer, or anything you want.

Comparing Fractions

Write >, <, or = in the circle to make a true math statement.

A. $\frac{2}{3} \bigcirc \frac{1}{3}$

B. $\frac{12}{13} \bigcirc \frac{11}{13}$

C. $\frac{1}{12} \bigcirc \frac{1}{3}$

D. $\frac{5}{9} \bigcirc \frac{6}{9}$

E. $\frac{2}{6} \bigcirc \frac{3}{6}$

F. $\frac{2}{5} \bigcirc \frac{4}{10}$

G. $\frac{1}{4} \bigcirc \frac{2}{8}$

H. $\frac{3}{4} \bigcirc \frac{1}{4}$

I. $\frac{3}{8} \bigcirc \frac{5}{8}$

Multiplication Facts for 9

Write the correct factor to complete each multiplication fact.

A. ☐ x 9 = 36

B. 3 x ☐ = 27

C. ☐ x 9 = 18

D.
```
  ☐
x 9
───
 54
```

E.
```
  5
  ☐
x
───
 45
```

F.
```
  ☐
x 9
───
 63
```

G. 1 x ☐ = 9

H. 2 x ☐ = 18

I. ☐ x 9 = 0

J. ☐ x 7 = 63

K. 9 x ☐ = 9

L. 9 x ☐ = 45

Alphabetical Order

Number the words in each group alphabetically from 1 to 5.
You will need to look all the way to the fourth or fifth letter in
each group before you start numbering.

1. _____ peanut
 _____ peacock
 _____ pear
 _____ peak
 _____ peat

2. _____ greet
 _____ greenhouse
 _____ grew
 _____ grenade
 _____ gremlin

3. _____ alligator
 _____ alley
 _____ allow
 _____ allude
 _____ allspice

4. _____ iceberg
 _____ icehouse
 _____ icebox
 _____ Iceland
 _____ icebreaker

Singular and Plural Possessives

Put an apostrophe in the correct position. Then, complete the sentence.

1. Several astronauts spacesuits _____ .

2. That boys football _____ .

3. The three poodles fur_____ .

4. The four cats claws_____ .

5. This weeks laundry basket _____ .

6. My three friends bikes _____ .

7. The suns rays _____ .

8. This robins nest _____ .

9. The elfs voice_____ .

10. The two beavers dams _____ .

Using Context Clues

When you come to a word you don't know, use the **context clues**, or other words around it, to help you figure out the meaning.

Use context clues to figure out the meaning of each highlighted word below. Circle the correct meaning.

1. The green light coming from the haunted house was frightening. It was an **eerie** sight!

 a. green **b.** spooky **c.** funny

2. We must leave soon. We must **depart** as soon as everyone is ready.

 a. watch **b.** leave **c.** sign

3. The **clasp** of the seat belt was not fastened correctly.

 a. buckle **b.** strap **c.** seat

Using Prefixes

A **prefix** is a syllable or syllables placed at the beginning of a base word to change its meaning. Here are some examples of prefixes:

un = not **re** = again **dis** = apart from, not

For each sentence, write a prefix that can be added to the highlighted word. Write the new word and its meaning.

1. I am **able** to do all of my work.

 prefix: _____ new word: _____

 meaning: _____

2. Mother will **agree** that my allowance should be more if I rake leaves.

 prefix: _____ new word: _____

 meaning: _____

Alphabetical Order

Number the names in each group alphabetically from 1 to 5.
Remember to alphabetize names by the **last** name.
Do you recognize any of these authors?

A. _____ Lewis Carroll

_____ Louisa May Alcott

_____ Mark Twain

_____ Hans Christian Andersen

_____ Charles Dickens

B. _____ Jules Verne

_____ Edgar Allan Poe

_____ J. R. R. Tolkien

_____ Robert Louis Stevenson

_____ Sir James Barrie

Working with Money

Read each problem and circle the correct answer.
Use extra paper to help you solve the problems if needed.

A. Jarvis has 5 quarters, 10 dimes, 3 nickels, and 37 pennies. How much money does he have?

$2.50 $2.67 $2.77 $3.77

B. Michael has $6.25. If he rents a video game for $4.75, how much change will he have?

$2.50 $2.75 $1.25 $1.50

C. Michelle wants to purchase an $11.00 baseball cap, a $15.00 shirt, and a $1.00 pack of gum. She has a $50.00 bill. How much change will she receive?

$27.00 $23.00 $77.00 $50.00

Diphthong ew

Use a word from the word list to complete each sentence correctly.

Word List

knew	chew	threw	blew	flew	view	review	newspaper

1. Be sure to _____ the last five chapters before the test.

2. Juan _____ the ball across the playground to Tony.

3. The _____ of the trees from the mountaintop was amazing.

4. I _____ Susan would like the birthday gift you bought for her.

5. The _____ is on the kitchen table.

6. Use your teeth to _____ your food.

7. I watched the bird as it _____ away.

8. The wind _____ the papers across the street.

Entry Words and Guide Words

Entry words are listed in the dictionary.
Guide words are words at the top of each page in the dictionary.

Look at each entry word and the guide words beside it. Decide if the entry word would come between the two guide words alphabetically in a dictionary. Write **yes** or **no** on the line.

	Entry Word	Guide Word	
1.	pyramid	puzzle, python	_____
2.	acrobat	acme, action	_____
3.	tutor	twinge, type	_____
4.	wrist	worsen, wrestle	_____
5.	blob	bleach, block	_____
6.	hummingbird	hunch, husky	_____
7.	crimson	crime, crocodile	_____
8.	fill	file, film	_____
9.	injure	inherit, ink	_____
10.	silver	silly, single	_____

Look at the guide words at the top of each word list below.
Circle only the words that would be entry words on a
dictionary page with those guide words.

A. lead–lease	B. crocus–crossing	C. gift–globe	D. rude–rummy
lean	cricket	giant	royal
leap	crop	give	ruler
left	croquet	glove	ruin
leaf	cross	glass	ruby

Review Multiplication Facts 6–9

Complete the multiplication facts. Do you see any patterns?

A. 6 x 0 = ____ 7 x 0 = ____ 8 x 0 = ____ 9 x 0 = ____

B. 6 x 1 = ____ 7 x 1 = ____ 8 x 1 = ____ 9 x 1 = ____

C. 6 x 2 = ____ 7 x 2 = ____ 8 x 2 = ____ 9 x 2 = ____

D. 6 x 3 = ____ 7 x 3 = ____ 8 x 3 = ____ 9 x 3 = ____

E. 6 x 4 = ____ 7 x 4 = ____ 8 x 4 = ____ 9 x 4 = ____

F. 6 x 5 = ____ 7 x 5 = ____ 8 x 5 = ____ 9 x 5 = ____

Diphthong oi

Use an **oi** word from the word list to complete each sentence.

Word List

voice
point
join
doily
soil
appoint
joint
boil
coin

1. My mother put a lace _____ on the table.

2. The elbow is a _____ in the arm.

3. The students had to _____ a class president.

4. Plant the seed in the _____.

5. I want to _____ the baseball team.

6. The singer had a lovely _____.

7. The change purse had only one _____ in it.

8. The water in the pot got so hot that it began to _____.

9. It is hard to write well with a pencil that has a dull _____.

Diphthong ou

Write each **ou** word from the word list under its rhyming word.
Circle the **ou** diphthong in each word.

Word List

scout		mound
	sound	
	sprout	
_____	pout	_____
	trout	
_____	stout	_____
	bound	
_____	round	_____
	about	
_____	surround	_____
	shout	
_____	pound	_____
	hound	

Review Multiplication Facts 6–9

Circle the correct product for each multiplication fact.

A. 6 x 7 =
42
12

B. 9 x 6 =
11
54

C. 4 x 6 =
24
16

D. 4 x 7¢ =
28¢
40¢

E. 8 x 8 =
40
64

F. 5 x 9¢ =
18¢
45¢

Definitions

Mary Martin, alias Peter Pan

Mary Martin is **fondly** remembered as the **petite** star who won an Emmy award for her **performance** in the TV production of *Peter Pan*. This cheerful, **exuberant** star was born Mary Virginia Martin on December 1, 1913. When she was 16, she married Benjamin Hagman. They had a son, Larry, who is **renowned** for his roles in the TV series *I Dream of Jeannie* and *Dallas*. Mary **exhibited** a talent for **aerial** ballet. After teaching and performing dance for several years, she **journeyed** to Hollywood to further her **career**. She had many **roles** in films and on Broadway.

Read the paragraph above carefully. Write the letter of the definition on the line next to each numbered word.

1. fondly _____
2. petite _____
3. performance _____
4. exuberant _____
5. renowned _____
6. roles _____
7. exhibited _____
8. aerial _____
9. journeyed _____
10. career _____

a. traveled

b. job, occupation

c. well known, famous

d. lovingly

e. enthusiastic

f. in the air

g. parts or characters played by an actor

h. small, little

i. the act of performing

j. showed or displayed

Constructing Stories

Write five sentences about the picture. Use the boxes at the end of each line to number your sentences in story order. Write your story and give it a title. Be sure to use capital letters and periods.

1. _____ ☐

2. _____ ☐

3. _____ ☐

4. _____ ☐

5. _____ ☐

Things to Think About
Who is this story about? Where does this story take place? How does this story begin? What happens next? How will this story end?

Reading a Table

A **table** is a compact, orderly arrangement of facts or figures, usually presented in rows or columns.

Use this table to answer the questions below.

Ross's Movie Rental Review

	Sun.	Mon.	Tues.	Wed.	Thurs.	Fri.	Sat.
Chuckie Chipmunk	1	4	0	2	3	5	2
Swamp Critters	2	3	1	2	0	2	3
Hero for a Day	0	6	2	1	4	5	5
Scary Vegetables	1	2	2	4	0	3	4
Halloween Howl	1	3	2	0	0	2	2

The numbers tell how many times each movie was rented each day.

1. Which movie was rented the most on Monday? _____

2. Which movie was rented the least on Monday? _____

3. Which movie was not rented on Tuesday? _____

4. Which movie was not rented on Wednesday or Thursday? _____

5. Were more movies rented on Saturday or Sunday? _____

6. Was *Chuckie Chipmunk* rented more than *Halloween Howl*? _____

7. On what day were the fewest movies rented? _____

8. Were more movies rented on Tuesday or Wednesday? _____

9. Which two days had seven movie rentals each? _____

10. How many times was *Swamp Critters* rented this week? _____

Math

Beat the Clock (Multiplication Facts Review)

A. $9 \times 1 =$ ___ $5 \times 8 =$ ___ $2 \times 5 =$ ___ $7 \times 5 =$ ___ $4 \times 7 =$ ___

B. $0 \times 5 =$ ___ $8 \times 0 =$ ___ $8 \times 6 =$ ___ $0 \times 9 =$ ___ $6 \times 3 =$ ___

C. $9 \times 6 =$ ___ $7 \times 4 =$ ___ $7 \times 0 =$ ___ $4 \times 4 =$ ___ $0 \times 3 =$ ___

D. $6 \times 4 =$ ___ $1 \times 7 =$ ___ $3 \times 7 =$ ___ $3 \times 1 =$ ___ $5 \times 3 =$ ___

E. $9 \times 9 =$ ___ $9 \times 3 =$ ___ $0 \times 4 =$ ___ $7 \times 9 =$ ___ $6 \times 0 =$ ___

F. $1 \times 3 =$ ___ $4 \times 8 =$ ___ $5 \times 7 =$ ___ $5 \times 2 =$ ___ $2 \times 1 =$ ___

G. $9 \times 4 =$ ___ $1 \times 0 =$ ___ $7 \times 1 =$ ___ $0 \times 0 =$ ___ $3 \times 6 =$ ___

H. $4 \times 3 =$ ___ $7 \times 8 =$ ___ $2 \times 4 =$ ___ $8 \times 5 =$ ___ $1 \times 2 =$ ___

I. $3 \times 8 =$ ___ $9 \times 8 =$ ___ $5 \times 1 =$ ___ $3 \times 0 =$ ___ $7 \times 3 =$ ___

J. $8 \times 1 =$ ___ $5 \times 6 =$ ___ $2 \times 0 =$ ___ $6 \times 2 =$ ___ $0 \times 8 =$ ___

K. $9 \times 7 =$ ___ $0 \times 1 =$ ___ $6 \times 6 =$ ___ $1 \times 6 =$ ___ $2 \times 9 =$ ___

L. $5 \times 0 =$ ___ $6 \times 9 =$ ___ $3 \times 2 =$ ___ $8 \times 0 =$ ___ $4 \times 0 =$ ___

M. $7 \times 2 =$ ___ $2 \times 6 =$ ___ $0 \times 7 =$ ___ $3 \times 5 =$ ___ $4 \times 6 =$ ___

N. $2 \times 3 =$ ___ $5 \times 9 =$ ___ $4 \times 2 =$ ___ $1 \times 1 =$ ___ $7 \times 7 =$ ___

O. $6 \times 5 =$ ___ $0 \times 6 =$ ___ $5 \times 5 =$ ___ $9 \times 2 =$ ___ $8 \times 2 =$ ___

P. $3 \times 9 =$ ___ $6 \times 1 =$ ___ $1 \times 5 =$ ___ $2 \times 8 =$ ___ $2 \times 2 =$ ___

Q. $1 \times 4 =$ ___ $1 \times 9 =$ ___ $4 \times 9 =$ ___ $0 \times 2 =$ ___ $6 \times 7 =$ ___

R. $8 \times 4 =$ ___ $4 \times 5 =$ ___ $7 \times 6 =$ ___ $9 \times 5 =$ ___ $5 \times 4 =$ ___

S. $8 \times 8 =$ ___ $6 \times 8 =$ ___ $9 \times 0 =$ ___ $3 \times 3 =$ ___ $8 \times 7 =$ ___

T. $3 \times 4 =$ ___ $4 \times 1 =$ ___ $2 \times 7 =$ ___ $8 \times 3 =$ ___ $1 \times 8 =$ ___

Time: _____ Number correct: _____

Remove pages 73–76. Cut along dashed lines. Staple pages in order.

Secret Codes and Puzzles

1

Use the secret code to solve the riddle.

What would your nose be if it were 12 inches long?

✦ ✚ ☛ ☛ ✳

Secret Code Key

✦ = A	☀ = G	✠ = L	◆ = Q	✦ = V	
✧ = B	✹ = H	☎ = M	✳ = R	✳ = W	
★ = C	✣ = I	♣ = N	✣ = S	▢ = X	
✪ = D	★ = J	☚ = O	✱ = T	● = Y	
☆ = E	✛ = K	✈ = P	✹ = U	◉ = Z	
✚ = F					

3

73

Use the secret code to solve the riddle.

What kind of house is the easiest to lift?

__ __ __ __ __ __ __ __ __ __ __
3 23 4 10 22 13 22 18 17 5 12

Secret Code Key

3 = A	23 = L	6 = Q	14 = V	
7 = B	10 = G	21 = R	2 = W	
11 = C	22 = H	20 = M	2 = W	
1 = D	4 = I	25 = N	5 = S	26 = X
12 = E	16 = J	18 = O	13 = T	14 = Y
15 = F	9 = K	24 = P	17 = U	8 = Z

Farmer Potter's cornfield is full of hungry crows. Find out if there are enough ears of corn on the page for each crow to have two ears. Circle the correct sentence below the picture.

There is enough corn for each crow to have two ears.

There is not enough corn for each crow to have two ears.

Use the secret code to solve the riddle.

What's worse than a giraffe with a sore throat?

$\overline{35}$ $\overline{15}$ $\overline{30}$ $\overline{5}$ $\overline{125}$ $\overline{10}$ $\overline{115}$ $\overline{30}$ $\overline{70}$ $\overline{30}$

$\overline{50}$ $\overline{10}$ $\overline{125}$ $\overline{45}$ $\overline{105}$ $\overline{80}$ $\overline{60}$ $\overline{30}$

$\overline{85}$ $\overline{30}$ $\overline{30}$ $\overline{125}$!

Secret Code Key

35 = A	110 = G	120 = L	100 = Q	130 = V
55 = B	45 = H	95 = M	60 = R	50 = W
15 = C	10 = I	5 = N	105 = S	65 = X
70 = D	75 = J	80 = O	125 = T	90 = Y
30 = E	40 = K	115 = P	20 = U	25 = Z
85 = F				

5

Help the hiker get back to his camp. Color the stones with multiples of 5. A path will appear to lead the hiker to his camp. The first and last stones are already marked.

7

75

Color a path across and down to move from start to finish. Each new square in the path must have a number greater than the previous number in the path. The first and last squares are already marked.

1	5	3	4	22	15	4
0	9	12	7	30	10	22
2	6	13	10	9	7	3
9	4	16	20	11	4	9
33	8	14	24	21	17	2
21	24	19	27	29	25	15
6	30	2	18	30	35	33
15	18	4	12	27	42	50

Use the secret code to solve the riddle.

What is yellow, weighs 1,000 pounds, and sings?

___ ___ ___ ___ - ___ ___ ___
27 54 75 51 3 69 45

___ ___ ___ ___ ___
72 45 24 57 42

___ ___ ___ ___ ___ ___ ___
9 24 57 42 66 51 42

___ ___ ___ ___ ___ ___ ___ ___
18 30 57 30 66 54 51 36

Secret Code Key

30 = A	15 = G	33 = L	39 = Q	75 = V
21 = B	9 = H	6 = M	66 = R	69 = W
18 = C	54 = I	57 = N	36 = S	48 = X
42 = D	78 = J	45 = O	3 = T	12 = Y
51 = E	60 = K	72 = P	24 = U	63 = Z
27 = F				

Multiplication Facts 0-9 Review

Problem List

9 x 1 = _9_

8 x 5 = ___ 5 x 8 = ___

7 x 5 = ___ 9 x 9 = ___

9 x 3 = ___ 3 x 8 = ___

7 x 7 = ___ 4 x 9 = ___

6 x 6 = ___ 3 x 6 = ___

7 x 4 = ___ 0 x 8 = ___

8 x 4 = ___ 9 x 4 = ___

9 x 2 = ___ 9 x 5 = ___

8 x 8 = ___ 9 x 7 = ___

Multiply to solve the problems in the problem list. Then, find the same problems in the puzzle. Circle the hidden problems and write **x** and **=** in the correct places. Problems are hidden across and down.

Compare and Contrast

Fill in the blanks with words that tell how a tree and flower are alike and different. The first ones have been done for you.

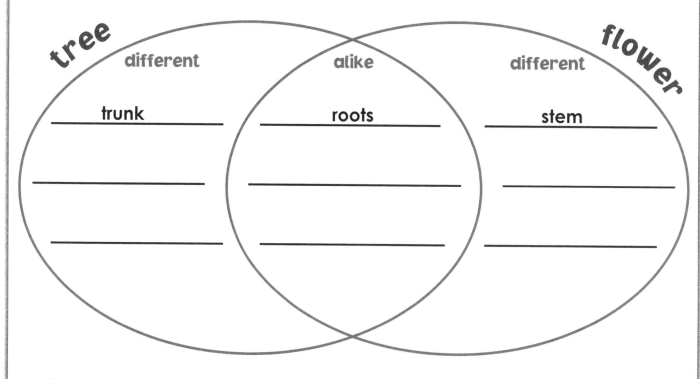

tree flower

different alike different

trunk roots stem

Write two paragraphs below. In the first paragraph, tell how trees and flowers are alike. Tell how each is different in the second paragraph. Give each paragraph a title.

_____ _____

_____ _____

_____ _____

_____ _____

_____ _____

_____ _____

Multiplying One- and Two-Digit Numbers

Rule:

Multiply ones, then regroup.
Multiply tens, then add extra tens.

Example:

```
  |        |
 23       23
x 6      x 6
———      ———
  8      138
```

Solve each problem. Write the answer in the space provided.

A. 10
x 5

B. 10
x 3

C. 12
x 2

D. 15
x 4

E. 19
x 2

F. 31
x 4

G. 62
x 2

H. 27
x 3

I. 54
x 3

J. 79
x 3

L. 87
x 5

M. 90
x 4

Diphthong ow

Write each word from the word list beside its rhyming word.
Circle the **ow** diphthong in each word on the line.

Word List

brow

powder

scowl

town

tower

prowl _____ _____

power _____ _____

bow _____ _____

down _____ _____

powder _____ _____

BONUS

Write another word with an **ow** diphthong to
rhyme with each word in the above activity.

79

Drawing Conclusions

Read the story. Then, answer the questions.

Photograph

Jack was not comfortable. His new shirt was too stiff and his tie felt tight. Mother had fussed over his hair trying to get it to look just right. She made him scrub his hands three times to get the dirt from under his fingernails! Finally, his mom said he was ready. She smiled and said that Jack looked very handsome. Jack frowned, but knew he could not tell his mom how he felt. This was important to her. Jack sat on a special stool that turned and looked at the camera. He didn't feel like smiling, but he did his best. "Perfect!" said the man behind the camera as he snapped the shot. Jack posed two more times, and then the man said they were finished. The first thing Jack did was take off his tie!

1. What was Jack doing?

2. What clues tell you where Jack is?

3. How does Jack feel about this?

4. What clues tell you how Jack feels?

5. Who was the man that said "perfect"?

6. Why did Jack take off his tie?

Counting Syllables

Syllables represent the number of vowel sounds heard in words.

Examples: what – 1 vowel sound and 1 syllable
pencil – 2 vowel sounds and 2 syllables
animal – 3 vowel sounds and 3 syllables

Read each word below. Use the line to write the number of syllables in the word. Listen to make sure that the number of vowel sounds equals the number of syllables for each word.

1. apple ____
2. prune ____
3. cherry ____

4. banana ____
5. lemon ____
6. pear ____

7. watermelon ____
8. plum ____
9. strawberry ____

Alphabetical Order

To alphabetize titles you need to put small words like **A**, **The**, or **An** at the end of a title.

Example: The Cat in the Hat would be Cat in the Hat, The.

Number the titles from 1 to 9 as they should appear alphabetically.

____ *Charlotte's Friend*
____ *Amos Goes Camping*
____ *The Chocolate Prize*
____ *Harvey's Mystery*
____ *The Whale Watchers*
____ *A Lion and a Bear*
____ *Where the River Ends*
____ *Cats for Sale*
____ *The Needlefish Return*

Multiplying One- and Three-Digit Numbers

Rule:

1. Multiply ones, then regroup.
2. Multiply tens, then add extra tens.
3. Multiply hundreds.
4. Regroup as needed.

Example:

```
  1          1          2 1
 453        453         453
x  4       x  4        x  4
---        ----        -----
  2         12         1,812
```

Solve the problems. Write the answers in the space provided.

A. 100
 x 3

B. 120
 x 2

C. 278
 x 4

D. 329
 x 3

E. 422
 x 5

F. 705
 x 4

G. 827
 x 9

H. 926
 x 7

Understanding What I Read

What Eats the Firefly?

There are very few animals that are not eaten by something. No creature, however, eats the firefly, or lightning bug. The adult firefly has almost no predators. Birds, insect-eating mammals, reptiles, and fish do not eat them. Sharks are also bothered by them. They will swish around wildly and then seem to be paralyzed with fear when fireflies are put in their tank.

Read the paragraph. Then, answer the questions.

1. What is the main idea of the paragraph? _____

2. What is another name for a firefly? _____

3. Describe what the fearless shark will do if a firefly is in its tank. _____

4. What do you think a predator is? _____

Reading a Bar Graph

This bar graph shows the different eye colors of the children in three third grade classes.

What Color Are Your Eyes?

Look at the graph and answer the following questions.

A. How many children have green eyes? _____

B. How many more children have blue eyes than gray eyes? _____

C. How many more children have brown eyes than blue eyes? _____

D. This graph lists eye color for how many third graders? _____

E. Which two eye colors are found in an equal number of students?

F. Make one statement about this graph based on the data given.

Diphthong oy

Look at the highlighted letters in each pair of words. Circle the word that is spelled correctly, and then use the word in a sentence.

1. enjoy enjoi _____

2. destroi destroy _____

3. loial loyal _____

4. royal roial _____

5. annoy annoi _____

6. toi toy _____

Multiplying Two- and Three-Digit Numbers

Rule:

1. Multiply ones by ones, tens, and hundreds. Regroup as needed.

2. Multiply tens by ones, tens, and hundreds. Regroup as needed.

3. Add the two numbers to find the final product.

Example:

```
  325        325         325
x  43      x  43       x  43
 975        975         975
           13000      +13000
                       13,975
```

Solve the problems.

A. 203 B. 330 C. 633 D. 567
 x 12 x 25 x 61 x 38

84

Multiplication Rounding and Estimating

Rule:
Since it is easier to multiply by numbers ending in 0, it can be useful to estimate an approximate answer by rounding.

Example:
26 x 9 = ___
26 rounds up to **30**,
so the estimated product is:
30 x **9** = **270**

Round the two-digit factor to the nearest ten.
Multiply to find the estimated product.

A. 18
 x 2

B. 23
 x 5

C. 15
 x 3

D. 24
 x 9

E. 58
 x 5

F. 64
 x 7

G. 75
 x 4

H. 81
 x 8

Adjectives

Use the line in front of each noun to
write an **adjective** that describes the noun.

1. _____ rain

2. _____ table

3. _____ flower

4. _____ day

5. _____ fruit

5. _____ petal

7. _____ grass

8. _____ friend

9. _____ lake

10. _____ house

Prefixes and Suffixes

Base Words	**Prefixes**	**Suffixes**
are the root words that are used to make other words.	are letters that are put in **front** of base words to change the meaning of the base words.	are letters added to the **end** of base words to change the meaning of the base word.
helpful	**rewrite**	**healthy**
The root word is **help**.	The prefix **re** changes the meaning of the base word **write**.	The suffix **y** changes the meaning of the base word **health**.

For each question below, decide which part of the word is highlighted in blue. Write **base word**, **prefix**, or **suffix** on the line.

1. punish**ment** _____

2. **dark**ness _____

3. dis**appear** _____

4. pre**cook** _____

5. **pre**soak _____

6. **proud**ly _____

7. **place**ment _____

8. dis**trust** _____

9. **color**less _____

10. friend**ly** _____

11. sick**ness** _____

12. sugar**less** _____

13. fool**ish** _____

14. brown**ish** _____

15. re**fill** _____

16. **re**pay _____

17. un**sure** _____

18. lone**ly** _____

Capitalization

In the story below, circle each letter that should be a capital letter.
Add an ending to the story.

my birthday

today is my birthday. i am nine years old. i was born on wednesday, april 12, in billings, montana. my family will celebrate my birthday tonight. mom will cook her special spaghetti dinner just for me. dad will be home from work early. my brother, david, and my sister, rose, will be here, too. after dinner grandma and grandpa will come. we will all eat cake and ice cream. they will sing "happy birthday" to me. then, i . . .

Fact and Opinion

A **fact** is something that is real and could happen.

An **opinion** is something that is believed to be true but may not be.

There are apples on the tree.

Those apples are beautiful.

Mark each sentence with an **F** for fact or an **O** for opinion.

_____ 1. My mother fixes dinner every night at 6:00.

_____ 2. Chocolate pie is the best dessert.

_____ 3. The state of Wisconsin is a part of the United States.

_____ 4. People can go to a movie theater to watch movies.

_____ 5. It is more fun to rent a movie and watch it at home than to go to a theater.

Math

Problem Solving with Multiplication

Solve the word problems. Show your work and write the answers in the space provided.

A. Sophia's Bakery sold 8 cakes each day for 21 days. How many cakes did the bakery sell in all?

B. Regina made 49 gift baskets each week for 5 weeks. Estimate how many gift baskets she made.

C. For 21 days of camp, Melanie collected 2 souvenirs each day. How many souvenirs did she collect in all?

D. Donna sold 136 bags of popcorn at the movie theater for 24 days. Estimate to find out about how many bags of popcorn Donna sold.

Classification

The words below all have something in common. What heading can you give the list that will name all the words? Write a heading on the line **Main Heading**. Sort the words in the box into two categories. Write the words on the lines. Write a subheading for each group.

big	bitty	enormous	fat	giant	gigantic
great	huge	large	little	long	mammoth
miniature	petite	short	skinny	slight	small
tall	teeny	thin	tiny	vast	wee

Main Heading

_____ _____

Subheading **Subheading**

Telling Time

Read each problem and circle the correct answer for each.

A. Which clock shows 8:30?

B. Which clock has the same time as the first one?

C. Which clock shows 15 minutes before 7?

D. **Quarter past four** is another way of saying which of the following times?

Beginning Digraphs: ch, sh, th

Say the name of each picture. Circle the beginning digraph.

1. ch th sh

2. ch th sh

3. ch th sh

4. ch th sh

Say the name of each picture. Write the beginning digraph **ch**, **sh**, or **th** to complete the word.

5. _____urch

6. _____icken

7. _____ell

8. _____imble

Beginning Digraph ph

Read the words. Underline the beginning digraph **ph** in each word.

1. physical 2. pharmacy 3. photograph

4. pharaoh 5. phantom 6. phonograph

7. physician 8. photosynthesis 9. phonics

Read the words. Circle each word that begins with the digraph **ph**.
Place an **x** on any word that does not begin with this digraph.

10. phony 11. photography 12. pinch 13. poetry

14. page 15. phobia 16. puddle 17. pharmacist

18. phase 19. please 20. piano 21. paper

Elapsed Time

Find each time. All times are a.m. Write the answer on the line provided.

A. 30 minutes after

B. 15 minutes after

C. 15 minutes after

D. 30 minutes after

E. 30 minutes before

F. 1 hour before

Reading a Calendar

Mrs. Simms has two children, Jay and Joy. The calendar shows
Jay's baseball games and Joy's soccer games in April.
Use the calendar to answer the questions.

April

Sunday	Monday	Tuesday	Wednesday	Thursday	Friday	Saturday
		1 Jay's game	2	3 Joy's game	4	5 Jay's & Joy's games
6	7 Jay's game	8 Joy's game	9	10 Joy's game	11	12 Joy's game
13 Jay's game	14	15 Jay's game	16	17 Joy's game	18	19 Jay's & Joy's games
20	21	22 Jay's game	23	24 Joy's game	25 Joy's game	26 Jay's game
27	28	29 Jay's game	30			

1. Who plays the first game of the month?

2. What day of the week is the first game?

3. Who has more games, Jay or Joy?

4. Who has a game on the second Tuesday of the month?

5. On April 24, Joy has a game. What day of the week is that?

6. How many games does Joy play on Tuesdays and Saturdays?

7. On which dates do both Jay and Joy have games?

8. A week begins on Sunday and ends on Saturday. In which week are the most games played?

9. Are there any days of the week in which no games are played?

Descriptive Writing

Read the following paragraph.

I have a favorite pair of shoes. They are old. My mom doesn't like them. She wants me to throw them away and get a new pair. I would rather keep my old shoes.

Now, read the same paragraph with adjectives and more description added.

I have a favorite pair of shoes. They are old and comfortable. The shoes are blue. The left shoe has a hole in the toe, and the right has a broken shoelace. Both of them have holes worn in the bottom. My mom doesn't like my old shoes. They are very dirty. She wants me to throw them away and get a new pair. I would rather keep my old, comfortable shoes.

Read the following paragraph. Then, rewrite it to make it more interesting using adjectives and more description.

Yesterday my family took a train ride. There were passenger cars, boxcars, and an engine. A caboose was at the end. The whistle blew. We were off! Smoke blew from the engine. The cars began to rock. I would like to ride on a train again.

Division Facts 0–1

Rules: 0 divided by any number will always equal 0.

Any number divided by 1 will always equal that number.

Examples: $0 \div 5 = 0$ $8 \div 1 = 8$

Solve each problem. Write the answer on the line.

A. $0 \div 12 =$ _____ **B.** $0 \div 10 =$ _____ **C.** $3 \div 1 =$ _____

D. $5 \div 1 =$ _____ **E.** $0 \div 3 =$ _____ **F.** $0 \div 6 =$ _____

G. $4 \div 1 =$ _____ **H.** $0 \div 9 =$ _____ **I.** $0 \div 1 =$ _____

J. $11 \div 1 =$ _____ **K.** $7 \div 1 =$ _____ **L.** $0 \div 2 =$ _____

M. $9 \div 1 =$ _____ **N.** $1 \div 1 =$ _____ **O.** $0 \div 8 =$ _____

Beginning Digraph qu

Say the name of each picture. Circle the picture if the word begins with the digraph **qu**. Put an **x** on the picture if the word does not begin with **qu**.

1. 2. 3. 4.

Read each word. If the word begins with the digraph **qu**, write **qu** on the line. If not, leave the line blank.

5. quarrel _____ **6.** quest _____ **7.** shadow _____

8. suntan _____ **9.** quiet _____ **10.** frown _____

11. quack _____ **12.** powder _____ **13.** quality _____

Prefixes and Suffixes

Divide the words below by separating the prefixes, suffixes, and base words.

Note: Sometimes the silent **e** is removed from the base word when a suffix is added. **Example:** remove – removable. Add the silent **e** to the base words that need it.

	Prefix	Base Word	Suffix
1. refreshment	re	fresh	ment
2. undependable			
3. enlargement			
4. unbelievable			
5. disappointment			
6. untruthful			
7. prearrangement			

Division Facts 2–4

Math

Rule:

10 items placed in groups of two equal 5 groups.

Example: =

Solve each problem. Write the answer on the line.

A. $16 \div 2 =$ _____ B. $8 \div 2 =$ _____ C. $4 \div 4 =$ _____

D. $14 \div 2 =$ _____ E. $24 \div 2 =$ _____ F. $48 \div 4 =$ _____

G. $12 \div 4 =$ _____ H. $36 \div 3 =$ _____ I. $36 \div 4 =$ _____

J. $22 \div 2 =$ _____ K. $18 \div 2 =$ _____ L. $20 \div 2 =$ _____

M. $20 \div 4 =$ _____ N. $15 \div 3 =$ _____ O. $2 \div 2 =$ _____

P. $28 \div 4 =$ _____ Q. $33 \div 3 =$ _____ R. $24 \div 3 =$ _____

Division Facts 1–5

Divide to solve the problems in the problem list. Then, find the same problems in the puzzle. Circle each hidden problem and write ÷ and = in the correct places. Problems are hidden across and down.

Problem List

6 ÷ 2 = __3__

4 ÷ 2 = _____

3 ÷ 3 = _____

15 ÷ 5 = _____

20 ÷ 5 = _____

25 ÷ 5 = _____

10 ÷ 2 = _____

8 ÷ 4 = _____

9 ÷ 3 = _____

20 ÷ 4 = _____

15 ÷ 3 = _____

12 ÷ 3 = _____

12 ÷ 4 = _____

5 ÷ 5 = _____

10 ÷ 5 = _____

8 ÷ 2 = _____

6 ÷ 3 = _____

16 ÷ 4 = _____

1	8	2	4	15	8	12	4	2	2	3
6	1	3	4	10	20	4	5	6	0	7
12	12	4	12	5	1	1	2	÷	5	2
3	3	16	4	2	16	15	6	2	8	6
6	4	1	3	1	4	3	9	=	3	5
3	8	4	2	3	4	5	1	3	0	5
2	1	15	3	7	20	2	20	8	4	1
7	16	5	2	25	5	5	3	5	20	3
11	6	3	4	7	9	2	5	1	9	4
8	1	5	1	10	2	5	3	5	1	8
10	7	12	3	10	4	8	1	3	3	3
3	6	2	5	2	1	6	25	2	6	2

Division Facts 5-7

Solve each problem. Then, write the answer on the line provided.

A. 30 ÷ 5 = _____ 54 ÷ 6 = _____ 49 ÷ 7 = _____

B. 12 ÷ 6 = _____ 15 ÷ 5 = _____ 60 ÷ 6 = _____

C. 40 ÷ 5 = _____ 28 ÷ 7 = _____ 25 ÷ 5 = _____

D. 18 ÷ 6 = _____ 70 ÷ 7 = _____ 60 ÷ 5 = _____

E. 42 ÷ 6 = _____ 63 ÷ 7 = _____ 77 ÷ 7 = _____

F. 35 ÷ 7 = _____ 7 ÷ 7 = _____ 14 ÷ 7 = _____

G. 48 ÷ 6 = _____ 36 ÷ 6 = _____ 10 ÷ 5 = _____

H. 20 ÷ 5 = _____ 55 ÷ 5 = _____ 84 ÷ 7 = _____

I. 56 ÷ 7 = _____ 45 ÷ 5 = _____ 66 ÷ 6 = _____

Ending Blend -mp

Add the ending blend **mp** to each set of letters. Say the words.

1. bu _____

2. ca _____

3. stu _____

4. lu _____

5. swa _____

6. shri _____

7. pu _____

8. cla _____

Look at each picture. Circle the **mp** word that
names each picture and write the word on the line.

9.

limp blimp skimp

10.

jump pump lump

11.

camp lamp ramp

Sequencing

Read the poem below to find out what was wrong with Buzzy's car.
Read the sentences next to the poem. Decide what happened first,
second, and so on. Number the sentences in the correct order.

Buzzy's New Car

Buzzy saved up all his money
To buy himself a car.
The one he bought looked kind of funny
And didn't take Buzzy far.

The first time out, a tire went flat,
And the radiator cracked in two.
Then the engine broke down after that.
Poor Buzzy didn't know what to do.

He pushed the car off the side of the road
And hoped somebody would stop.
Buzzy was mad—enough to explode—
Then the other tire went, "POP!"

Now Buzzy's still sitting beside that old heap.
His hair all turned gray and grew long.
This one is a car nobody would keep.
Since everything on it went wrong!

_____ Buzzy's hair turned gray.

_____ The engine broke down.

_____ Buzzy bought a car.

_____ A second tire went "POP!"

_____ Buzzy saved his money.

_____ The radiator cracked.

_____ Buzzy pushed the car off the road.

Division Facts 8-9

Solve each problem. Write the answer on the line provided.

A. $16 \div 8 =$ _____ $24 \div 8 =$ _____ $54 \div 9 =$ _____

B. $36 \div 9 =$ _____ $72 \div 9 =$ _____ $56 \div 8 =$ _____

C. $88 \div 8 =$ _____ $32 \div 8 =$ _____ $72 \div 8 =$ _____

D. $45 \div 9 =$ _____ $81 \div 9 =$ _____ $80 \div 8 =$ _____

E. $27 \div 9 =$ _____ $90 \div 9 =$ _____ $96 \div 8 =$ _____

F. $40 \div 8 =$ _____ $64 \div 8 =$ _____ $63 \div 9 =$ _____

G. $8 \div 8 =$ _____ $18 \div 9 =$ _____ $108 \div 9 =$ _____

H. $48 \div 8 =$ _____ $9 \div 9 =$ _____ $99 \div 9 =$ _____

Division Facts 1-9

Divide to solve the problems and then color.

4 = red 7 = orange
5 = purple 8 = yellow
6 = green 9 = black

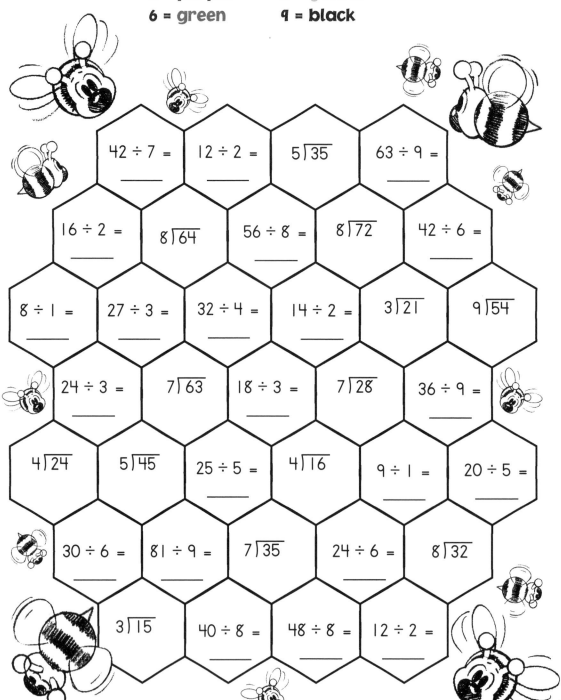

42 ÷ 7 = ___

12 ÷ 2 = ___

5⟌35

63 ÷ 9 = ___

16 ÷ 2 = ___

8⟌64

56 ÷ 8 = ___

8⟌72

42 ÷ 6 = ___

8 ÷ 1 = ___

27 ÷ 3 = ___

32 ÷ 4 = ___

14 ÷ 2 = ___

3⟌21

9⟌54

24 ÷ 3 = ___

7⟌63

18 ÷ 3 = ___

7⟌28

36 ÷ 9 = ___

4⟌24

5⟌45

25 ÷ 5 = ___

4⟌16

9 ÷ 1 = ___

20 ÷ 5 = ___

30 ÷ 6 = ___

81 ÷ 9 = ___

7⟌35

24 ÷ 6 = ___

8⟌32

3⟌15

40 ÷ 8 = ___

48 ÷ 8 = ___

12 ÷ 2 = ___

Writing Paragraphs

Choose an idea for your paragraph. Write the title, main idea, and details. Retell the main idea at the end.

Title of Paragraph

Main Idea

Details
1.
2.
3.
4.

Retell Main Idea

Use the sentences above to write a paragraph. Write the main idea, add the details, and retell the main idea. Indent the first sentence. Use capital letters and periods. Remember to give the paragraph a title.

Using a Thesaurus

A **thesaurus** is a book containing words listed alphabetically.
Beside the words are synonyms for the words. When you are writing a
report or working on a project and you have used a word too often, you
can turn to a thesaurus for another word that means the same thing.

Example: catch—grasp, grip, clutch, seize, take,
snatch, capture, clasp

Find other words that you can substitute for each word below.
Think of your own words before you turn to your thesaurus.

1. win _____

2. admire _____

3. vanish _____

4. bright _____

5. thin _____

6. calm _____

7. sleep _____

8. big _____

9. work _____

10. rare _____

Beat the Clock (Division Facts 1-9)

A.

$5\overline{)10}$ $4\overline{)28}$ $2\overline{)4}$ $9\overline{)63}$ $6\overline{)30}$ $4\overline{)16}$ $9\overline{)0}$ $3\overline{)15}$ $8\overline{)72}$ $6\overline{)18}$

B.

$8\overline{)48}$ $3\overline{)6}$ $7\overline{)21}$ $1\overline{)3}$ $7\overline{)56}$ $6\overline{)0}$ $2\overline{)16}$ $6\overline{)54}$ $1\overline{)7}$ $9\overline{)45}$

C.

$7\overline{)49}$ $5\overline{)35}$ $3\overline{)24}$ $7\overline{)7}$ $3\overline{)12}$ $8\overline{)24}$ $1\overline{)1}$ $9\overline{)72}$ $7\overline{)35}$ $5\overline{)25}$

D.

$9\overline{)27}$ $1\overline{)0}$ $8\overline{)40}$ $5\overline{)15}$ $2\overline{)2}$ $6\overline{)48}$ $5\overline{)0}$ $4\overline{)24}$ $2\overline{)8}$ $5\overline{)15}$

E.

$7\overline{)49}$ $6\overline{)12}$ $3\overline{)3}$ $2\overline{)12}$ $9\overline{)9}$ $1\overline{)5}$ $6\overline{)24}$ $4\overline{)4}$ $8\overline{)64}$ $5\overline{)45}$

F.

$2\overline{)6}$ $6\overline{)24}$ $4\overline{)12}$ $3\overline{)0}$ $8\overline{)8}$ $4\overline{)36}$ $2\overline{)0}$ $7\overline{)28}$ $9\overline{)63}$ $3\overline{)21}$

G.

$6\overline{)42}$ $7\overline{)35}$ $1\overline{)8}$ $9\overline{)54}$ $3\overline{)27}$ $4\overline{)0}$ $5\overline{)5}$ $5\overline{)40}$ $1\overline{)4}$ $7\overline{)0}$

H.

$4\overline{)32}$ $2\overline{)18}$ $9\overline{)81}$ $8\overline{)56}$ $3\overline{)9}$ $1\overline{)3}$ $2\overline{)14}$ $9\overline{)36}$ $4\overline{)8}$ $8\overline{)16}$

I.

$7\overline{)14}$ $8\overline{)48}$ $5\overline{)20}$ $6\overline{)6}$ $1\overline{)2}$ $8\overline{)0}$ $5\overline{)30}$ $7\overline{)56}$ $1\overline{)9}$ $8\overline{)32}$

J.

$1\overline{)6}$ $6\overline{)54}$ $6\overline{)36}$ $3\overline{)18}$ $7\overline{)63}$ $4\overline{)8}$ $2\overline{)10}$ $7\overline{)42}$ $9\overline{)18}$ $4\overline{)20}$

Time: **Number correct:**

Ending Blend -nd

Look at the pictures and say the words.
Circle the **nd** word that names each picture.

1.

2.

3.

sand fond wand | land stand round | bond band bend

Read each sentence. Circle the **nd** word that completes the sentence.

4. We left at the _____ of the movie. land end suspend
5. Be careful when you _____ on the stool. remind stand hand
6. I saw a penny on the _____. wind send ground
7. Guide dogs help the _____. blind spend fund

Decimal Place Value

Rule:

The decimal point separates the ones digit from the tenths digit.

Example:

23.45 = **2** **3** **4** **5**

 tens ones • tenths hundredths

Underline the digit in the tenths place.

A. 38.15 **B.** 11.18 **C.** 65.56 **D.** 50.63

E. 10.93 **F.** 9.95 **G.** 19.81 **H.** 19.58

Underline the digit in the hundredths place.

I. 19.62 **J.** 6.78 **K.** 73.17 **L.** 35.18

M. 25.84 **N.** 22.15 **O.** 99.99 **P.** 18.33

Proofreading

Add punctuation marks and capital letters where they are needed in the story below. Add an ending to the story.

the mother bird was busy with her three new babies they were growing so quickly soon they would begin flying they were always hungry she could never seem to find enough food to keep them full back and forth she flew all day long with worms and bugs

chirpy was the smallest of the three babies he was also the bravest he liked to jump to the edge of the nest to see his new world the mother bird warned him to be careful she said that he might fall from the nest there were cats in the yard below how would he get home if he fell out of the nest

the mother bird flew away to get the babies their dinner chirpy hopped right up on the edge of the nest suddenly his foot slipped he began to fall and . . .

Finish the Story

Hannah loved monster movies. She would stay up all night to watch them. One night when there was school the next day, Hannah sneaked downstairs to watch a monster movie at three o'clock in the morning. She was very tired when she went back to bed. When her alarm went off an hour later, Hannah got up and looked in the mirror.

"Oh, no!" she said, for now she was big and green and scaly and horrible. Hannah had turned into a monster herself.

Write what happened next.

Vocabulary Assessment

Read the first part of each sentence. Choose the word that means about the same thing as the highlighted word or phrase.
Fill in the circle next to the correct answer.

1. To **wash or clean by rubbing hard** is to . . .

 ○ dimple
 ○ crumble
 ○ scrub

2. A **group of related sentences** is a . . .

 ○ paragraph
 ○ sniffle
 ○ mission

3. When you **get something**, you . . .

 ○ reappear
 ○ navigate
 ○ receive

4. The **smallest amount** is the . . .

 ○ rate
 ○ mutter
 ○ least

5. Two things that are **completely different** are called . . .

 ○ onward
 ○ opposite
 ○ mischief

6. To be **thankful** is to be . . .

 ○ necessary
 ○ sloppy
 ○ grateful

7. Anything that **happened before now** is the . . .

 ○ future
 ○ past
 ○ native

8. A **book that lists meanings** of words is a . . .

 ○ marvel
 ○ represent
 ○ dictionary

9. When you **stay behind**, you . . .

 ○ remain
 ○ hitch
 ○ express

10. To **make a person do something he doesn't want to do** is to . . .

 ○ force
 ○ outwit
 ○ link

Grammar

Compound Words

Finish the story below using the words in the word bank. Write the compound words in the blanks where they belong.

| backyard | fireflies | lonesome | moonlight | waterproof |
| campfire | flashlight | midnight | rattlesnake | weekend |

Camping

Last _____ I went camping. I had a _____

tent in case it rained. It was great fun at first. The _____ were

glowing in the bushes. I built a warm _____. The

_____ was so bright I didn't even need my _____!

About _____, I became _____ and a little scared. I

thought I heard a _____ near my tent. Thank goodness I was

in my own _____!

Grammar

Parts of Speech

Read each sentence. List each word on the line beside the correct part of speech.

1. These berries smash easily.

noun _____ adjective _____
verb _____ adverb _____

2. Ten soldiers march together.

noun _____ adjective _____
verb _____ adverb _____

3. The big pillow belongs here.

noun _____ adjective _____
verb _____ adverb _____

Reading and Writing Decimals

Decimals are numbers used to represent fractions. They contain a decimal point. Change the numbers below from word form to decimals.

Example: six and five-tenths is written **6.5**

A. two-tenths _____

B. five-tenths_____

C. seven-hundredths _____

D. one and nine-hundredths_____

E. four and six-tenths _____

F. fifteen and eight-hundredths_____

Ending Blends: -lk, -nk, -sk

Say the name of each picture. Circle the word that names the picture and underline the ending.

1.	2.	3.
trunk / silk / task	yolk / sank / desk	walk / bank / ask

Circle the ending blend in each word.

4. k i o s k 5. f o l k 6. h u s k 7. t h i n k

8. f r i s k 9. w i n k 10. s u l k 11. b l i n k

12. t a l k 13. y a n k 14. b r i s k 15. s k u l k

Cause and Effect

A **cause** is the reason something happens.
An **effect** is what happens.

Example:
The cat scratched me because I pulled its tail.
Cause—I pulled its tail.
Effect—The cat scratched me.

Underline the **cause** in each sentence.

1. The rain started, and the boys ran for shelter.

2. Mother served ice cream and cake after dinner because it is my favorite dessert.

3. Since I cannot swim, my dad will not let me go to the lake by myself.

4. Joshua sleeps most of the day because he is a baby.

5. Mary cannot go to school because she is sick.

Circle the **effect** in each sentence.

6. Noel went to the movies this afternoon because she was bored.

7. I was so tired that I went to bed early last night.

8. Since she had work to do, Anna did not watch television today.

9. I made an A on my test because I studied.

10. I skinned my knee when I fell off my bike.

Crossword Puzzles

1

Use the word list to solve the crossword puzzle.

Word List

dragon	moat	queen
knight	armor	jester
king	castle	farmers

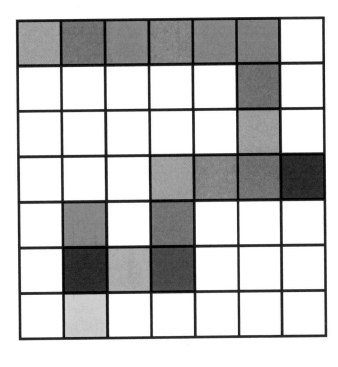

Across

4. _____ were people who grew food for the king.
5. A _____ carried a sword and served the king.
7. A _____ was a legendary fire-breathing creature.

Down

1. The wife of the king was called the _____.
2. A _____ amused the king by clowning and joking.
3. The king's large stone home was called a _____.
5. The ruler of the land was called the _____.
6. The water-filled area that surrounded the castle was called the _____.
8. A metal suit worn by a knight was called _____.

3

111

Use the word list to solve the crossword puzzle.

Word List

growl	cave
forest	claws
hibernate	grizzly
cubs	teddy

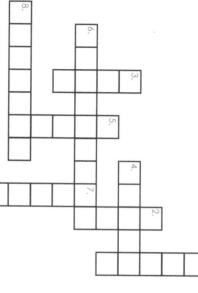

Across

4. Bears have sharp ____.
6. Bears sleep, or ____, all winter.
8. A large brownish bear found in North America is a ____.

Down

1. A wooded place where bears live is a ____.
2. A bear might make its home in a ____.
3. Baby bears are called ____.
5. A ____ is a noise a bear makes.
7. A toy bear with stuffing inside is called a ____ bear.

2

Use the word list to solve the crossword puzzle.

Word List

dessert
waiter
meals
chef
restaurant
salad
napkin
beverage
utensils

Across

5. A place to go out to eat is a ____.
8. Chocolate cake is my favorite ____.
9. Wipe your mouth with a ____.

Down

1. The ____ works in the kitchen preparing meals.
2. Breakfast, lunch, and dinner are all ____.
3. I like ranch dressing on my ____.
4. Knives, forks, and spoons are all ____.
6. A ____ takes orders in a restaurant.
7. Another word for drink is ____.

4

112

Use the word list to solve the crossword puzzle.

Word List

pool
water
goggles
raft
ocean
bubbles
kick
dive
stroke
splash

Across
2. Swimmers use their legs to _____.
4. A person wears _____ over his eyes to help him see underwater.
7. Air _____ float to the surface of the water.
9. A _____ can be used to ride on the waves.
10. The large body of water at the beach is called the _____.

Down
1. You _____ into the water when you jump head first.
3. A large container with water for swimming is called a _____.
5. A swimmer's arm motion is called a _____.
6. Don't dive into the pool if you don't know the depth of the _____.
8. Jumping into water causes a _____.

5

Use the word list to solve the crossword puzzle.

Word List

hail
clouds
sunshine
fog
rain
storm
wind
thunder
tornado
blizzard

Across
2. The _____ feels warm.
3. Wind along with rain, thunder, and lightning is usually called a _____.
6. It's snowing so hard I can't see. This is called a _____.
8. Water falling from the sky is _____.
9. March is a month with strong _____.
10. A cloud near the ground that is hard to see through is called _____.

Down
1. Boom! It must be _____.
4. A funnel of wind is called a _____.
5. Before a storm, you usually see many _____.
7. Rain in the form of small, frozen pellets is _____.

7

113

Use the word list to solve the crossword puzzle.

Word List

beach	sand
tide	seashore
fish	seaweed
reef	coral
ocean	shells

Across

3. Another name for the coast is the _____.
5. A marine animal that looks like a colorful rock is _____.
6. Many people like to walk along the beach and collect _____.
7. A _____ is a ridge of rock or coral near the surface of the water.
8. The rise and fall of the sea is called the _____.

Down

1. Many different types of _____ swim in the sea.
2. A _____ is covered with sand.
3. _____ is a plant that grows in the ocean.
4. A large body of salt water is called an _____.
6. The beach is made of tiny grains of rock called _____.

6

Use the word list to solve the crossword puzzle.

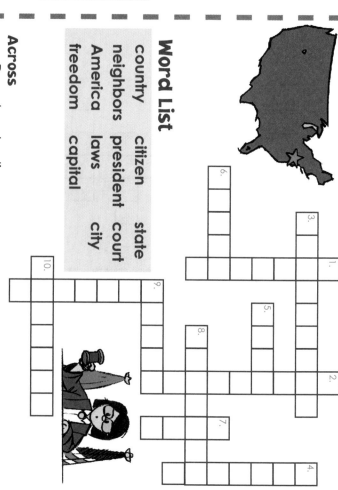

Word List

country	citizen	state
neighbors	president	court
America	laws	city
freedom	capital	

Across

3. People who live near you are your _____.
5. Rules that all citizens must follow are called _____.
6. Each star on the U.S. flag represents one _____.
8. U.S.A. stands for the United States of _____.
9. A judge hears trials in a _____.
10. Personal _____ means that citizens can make their own decisions.

Down

1. A person born in the U.S. is called a _____ of the country.
2. The chief executive of the U.S. is the _____.
4. The city that is the center of government is the _____.
7. A population center within a state is called a _____.
9. Another name for a nation is _____.

8

114

Adverbs

An **adverb** is a word that describes a verb. Adverbs tell **where, when, how**, or **to what extent** (how much, how long, or how often).

Examples: You can have a snack **later**. (When?)
Are there cookies **here?** (Where?)
Mom makes cookies **easily**. (How?)
I **never** eat potato chips. (How often?)

Use your imagination to complete the story with adverbs.
Remember, adverbs tell when, where, how, or to what extent.

News travels _____ in my school. On the

day I won 100 ice-cream cone coupons, _____

everybody was my friend. Marty came _____

up to me. She begged me for a chocolate cone. I told her _____

_____ that I would think about it. Fernando came

_____. He got _____ on

his knees and begged _____. Jill offered to

trade me her bubble gum for a strawberry ice cream coupon, but

I said, "No, thanks." Wow, people sure act _____

sometimes. I _____ do want to share my ice

cream, I just want to wait _____.

Ending Blends: -ft, -nt, -st

Say the name of each picture.
Write the ending blends, **ft**, **nt**, or **st,** to complete the word.

1. li _____	**2.** fore _____	**3.** te _____	**4.** pla _____
5. a _____	**6.** wri _____	**7.** gi _____	**8.** ne _____

Adding and Subtracting Decimals

Rule:
1. Line up the decimal points.
2. Start from the far right.
3. Regroup as needed.
4. Bring the decimal point down to the answer.

Example:

3.76 + 1.59 =

```
         1 1        1 1
  3.76   3.76      3.76
+ 1.59 + 1.59    + 1.59
         5 3 5    5.35
```

A. 6.5 + 7.3	**B.** 2.7 + 4.1	**C.** 6.5 − 1.2	**D.** 5.9 − 2.5
E. 12.5 + 9.4	**F.** 0.42 + 0.36	**G.** 2.41 + 7.49	**H.** 5.7 + 8.5
I. 3.8 + 4.9	**J.** 10.5 − 7.7	**K.** 4.13 − 2.95	**L.** 0.28 + .87

Persuasive Paragraphs

You must convince your mom to let you play in the rain.
Give your reasons. Then, ask again.

Title	
Question	May I . . .
Reasons	1.
	2.
	3.
	4.
Ask again	

Use the sentences above to write a paragraph. Ask the question, state the reasons, and then ask the question again. Indent the first sentence. Use capital letters and periods. Remember to give your paragraph a title.

Syllables

Find out how many syllables are in each word by counting the number of vowels you hear when you say the word. Write the number on the blank.

1. machine _____ 2. somersault _____ 3. peanut _____

4. neighborhood _____ 5. astronaut _____ 6. koala _____

7. dragon _____ 8. itch _____ 9. hero _____

10. auditorium _____ 11. longitude _____ 12. congratulate _____

13. frog _____ 14. multiplication _____ 15. Canada _____

16. zipper _____ 17. gulf _____ 18. lasagna _____

Adding and Subtracting Fractions

Rule:
When adding or subtracting fractions with the same denominator:

Examples: $\frac{3}{8} + \frac{2}{8} = \frac{8}{8}$

1. Add or subtract their numerators.
2. Write that number over the same denominator.

$\frac{9}{10} - \frac{3}{10} = \frac{6}{10}$

Solve each problem. Write the answer in the space provided.

A. $\frac{4}{7} - \frac{2}{7} =$

B. $\frac{1}{3} + \frac{1}{3} =$

C. $\frac{7}{8} - \frac{5}{8} =$

D. $\frac{3}{11} + \frac{5}{11} =$

E. $\frac{10}{25} - \frac{3}{25} =$

F. $\frac{1}{5} - \frac{1}{5} =$

Writing Stories

Write a story about the picture. Be sure to use capital letters
and periods where needed. Give your story a title.

Things to Think About

Who is this story about?

Where does this story take place?

How does the story begin?

What happens next?

How will the story end?

Division

Example:

$$6\overline{)30}$$
$$\underline{-30}$$
$$0$$

quotient: 5

Think:

6 divides evenly into 30, leaving no remainder.

Solve the problems.

A. $5\overline{)35}$

B. $7\overline{)14}$

C. $4\overline{)28}$

D. $3\overline{)24}$

E. $3\overline{)18}$

F. $8\overline{)56}$

G. $3\overline{)33}$

H. $8\overline{)64}$

Synonyms

Synonyms are words that have the same or almost the same meaning.
Examples: work – toil, small – little

Circle the two words in each row that are synonyms.

1.	beautiful	clever	pretty	eager
2.	wicked	evil	curious	calm
3.	hymn	honor	fall	respect
4.	sing	volley	clap	applaud
5.	get	return	area	receive
6.	unhappy	tender	shock	sad
7.	end	plead	beg	cause

Ending Digraphs: -ch, -sh, -th

Say the name of each picture.
Circle the word that names the picture and write the word.

1.

much

which

couch

2.

brush

wish

dish

3.

broth

with

mouth

4.

wreath

bath

sloth

5.

teach

peach

beach

6.

rush

bush

ash

Division with No Remainders

Example:

```
     1 2
4 ) 4 8
   - 4
    0 8
    - 8
      0
```

Think:

4 divides evenly into 48, leaving no remainder.

Solve the problems.

A. 2)64

B. 9)90

C. 6)72

D. 4)100

E. 3)69

F. 3)36

G. 6)84

H. 5)125

Division with Remainders

Example:

$$4\overline{)35} \quad \begin{array}{r} 8\,R3 \\ -32 \\ \hline 3 \end{array}$$

Think:

35 divided by 4 is 8 because 8 x 4 is closest to 35 without exceeding 35.

Then, 35 – 32 is 3, and 3 is called the remainder.

Solve the problems.

A. $4\overline{)75}$

B. $6\overline{)63}$

C. $9\overline{)98}$

D. $7\overline{)87}$

E. $3\overline{)52}$

F. $8\overline{)89}$

G. $3\overline{)34}$

H. $2\overline{)39}$

Ending Digraph -ng

Read the **ng** words. Circle the ending digraph and draw a line from each word to its description.

1. b a n g
2. f a n g
3. r i n g
4. w i n g

A. a piece of jewelry worn on the finger
B. the part of a bird that helps it fly
C. a sharp, pointy tooth
D. a loud noise

Look at the pictures and say the **ng** words.
Circle the **ng** word that names each picture.

5.

hang gong sing

6.

wrong king long

7.

swing lung strong

Ending Digraph -dge

Read the words. Circle each word that ends with the digraph **dge**.

1. sludge
2. clay
3. partridge
4. insect

5. ridge
6. wade
7. fudge
8. age

9. lodge
10. hedge
11. sled
12. ride

Look at the pictures and say the words. Fill in the circle
next to the **dge** word that names each picture.

13.

○ badge

○ edge

14.

○ judge

○ fudge

15.

○ lodge

○ bridge

Problem Solving with Division

Solve the problems. Show your work.

A. Stan had 32 bags of popcorn to sell at the snack bar. He sold all of the popcorn to 8 customers. If each customer bought the same number of popcorn bags, how many bags did each buy?

B. Ms. Davis drove 325 miles in 5 days. If she drove the same number of miles each day, how many miles did she drive?

C. Phil sold 146 magazine subscriptions. He worked for 2 weeks and sold the same amount each week. How many subscriptions did he sell each week?

D. Reginald has 162 seeds to plant in his garden. If he digs 18 holes in the soil and wants to distribute the seeds equally, how many seeds can he put in each hole?

Problem Solving with Decimals

A. Complete the next 3 decimals in each sequence.

.15, .25, .35, .45, ____ ____ ____

3.8, 3.7, 3.6, 3.5, ____ ____ ____

B. Using the greater than (>) and less than (<) symbols, write two number sentences using the following numbers: **3.4, 3.5**

C. Place the following numbers in order from least to greatest.

2.5, 5.2, 4.2, 4.12, 5.25

_____, _____, _____, _____, _____

D. Chuck's weekly allowance is $5.00. After buying a package of beef jerky for $1.67, how much money does he have left?

Antonyms

Antonyms are words that have opposite meanings.
Examples: hot – cold, near – far

Circle the two words in each row that are antonyms.

1.	juggle	approve	explode	dislike
2.	grasp	fact	achieve	fail
3.	sure	blot	calm	stormy
4.	even	escape	plain	uneven
5.	wrong	call	wait	right
6.	shame	honor	helpful	below

Sequencing

Sequencing means to put things in the proper order.

The hot chocolate recipe in the box is all mixed up.
After reading all the steps, put the recipe in the correct order.
Some steps have already been written.

Hot Chocolate for Cold Days

Pour a cup of water into a pan and heat it until it is boiling.

Put 3 tablespoons of hot chocolate mix into the mug.

Pour the heated water into the mug and stir.

Place a marshmallow on top and drink.

Turn off the stove and remove the hot water.

Take out a mug, spoon, and hot chocolate mix and set aside.

1. Take out a mug, spoon, and hot chocolate mix and set aside.

2. _____

3. Put 3 tablespoons of hot chocolate mix into the mug.

4. Turn off the stove and remove the hot water.

5. _____

6. _____

Graphic Art Project

Follow the directions below to make a colorful drawing.

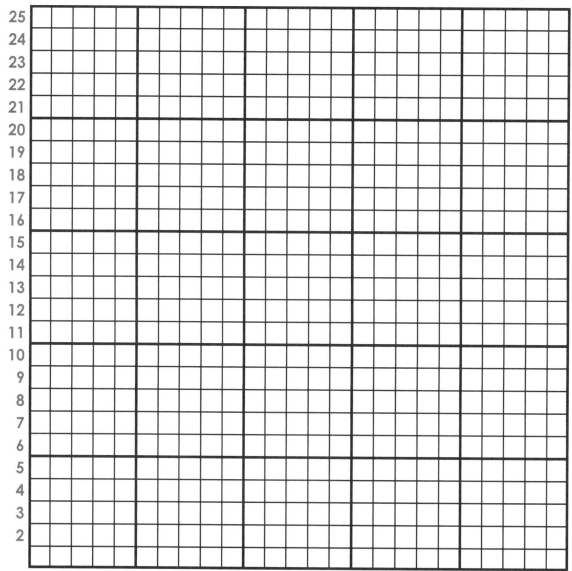

1. Color these boxes yellow: (10, 18) (10, 19) (10, 20) (9, 19) (11, 19) (8, 10)
2. Color these boxes red: (8, 1) (12, 1) Then, color the boxes between them red.
3. Color these boxes red: (12, 6) (12, 7) (13, 6) (13, 7) (9, 13)
4. Color these boxes brown: (9, 2) (10, 2) (11, 2) (9, 3) (10, 3) (11, 3)
5. Color these boxes blue: (10, 8) (10, 15)
6. Color these boxes orange: (6, 6) (7, 6) (6, 7) (7, 7) (11, 10) (12, 10) (11, 11) (12, 11)
7. Color these boxes green: (2, 4) (18, 4) Then, color the boxes between them green.
8. Color these boxes green: (3, 5) (3, 6) (4, 7) (4, 8) (5, 9) (5, 10) (6, 11) (6, 12) (7, 13)
 (7, 14) (8, 15) (8, 16) (9, 17) (10, 17) (11, 17) (12, 16) (12, 15)
 (13, 14) (13, 13) (14, 12) (14, 11) (15, 10) (15, 9) (16, 8) (16, 7)
 (17, 6) (17, 5)
9. Color the rest of the picture any way you want.

It's Me!

By _____

1

My name is _____ .

Here are some words that I
can make from the letters of my name:

Some interesting facts about my name:

3

About the Author

This book is dedicated to _____

2

I Am Me!

I am unique, I'm one-of-a-kind.
My face, my body, and my mind
Are all special parts of me.
And there's no one else I'd rather be.
I like who I am, I certainly do.
I'm a special someone, I know it's true.
I am proud and happy to know
That I am ME from head to toe!

I am special because _____

Here are adjectives that describe me:

4

The _____ Family

This is how we look:

My Family

5

My future is full of endless possibilities.
I hope that when I grow up I can . . .

When I grow up, I think I will
look like this:

7

129

Page 6

There's nothing like a good friend.
Some of my good friends are . . .

My friends and I like to _____

Here's a picture of my best friend:

Page 8

I can make today a happy day by . . .

Silent Letter in "tch"

Read the words. If the word ends with the digraph **tch**,
fill in the circle and circle the ending digraph.

1. ○ p i t c h 2. ○ s e a r c h 3. ○ h u t c h 4. ○ f i g h t
5. ○ w i t h 6. ○ s u c h 7. ○ w r a t h 8. ○ t w i t c h
9. ○ p a t c h 10. ○ h a t c h 11. ○ f e t c h 12. ○ c l u t c h

Say the name of each picture. Circle the word that names the picture.

13.

hatch watch catch

14.

stretch itch blotch

15.

batch crutch stitch

Perimeter

Math

Perimeter is the measurement of the length around a figure.
You can find the perimeter by adding the lengths of all the sides.

Look at the following figures and find the perimeter of each.

A.

Perimeter = _____ units

B.

Perimeter = _____ units

Subject-Verb Agreement

Complete each sentence with the correct verb form.

1. In the summer, I _____ as a detective.
(work / works)

2. I _____ neighborhood mysteries.
(solve / solves)

3. When Mrs. Carter _____ her cat, I help her find it.
(lose / loses)

4. If there are footprints, I _____ out whose they are.
(find / finds)

5. My friend Jim _____ me secret messages.
(write / writes)

6. I _____ my decoder to figure them out.
(use / uses)

7. I _____ my detective kit in a secret place.
(keep / keeps)

8. Only Mom and Dad _____ where it is.
(know / knows)

Predicting

Read the paragraph. Then answer the questions.

The children were playing baseball in the empty lot. Peggy was at bat. She swung hard and hit the ball farther than anyone else had. The ball sailed across the lot and smashed through Mrs. Allen's window. Peggy knew Mrs. Allen would be really angry. The other kids scattered, running for home. Peggy looked at the broken window.

1. What do you think Peggy will do?

2. Which clues helped you to decide?

Metric Length

Rules:

1 centimeter (cm) = 10 millimeters (mm)
1 decimeter (dm) = 10 centimeters
1 meter (m) = 100 centimeters
1 kilometer (km) = 1,000 meters

Example:

Is 1 m longer than 120 cm?
1 m = 100 cm, so 1 meter is not longer than 120 cm.
Answer: No

Answer each question. Write **yes** or **no** on the line provided.

A. Is 15 cm longer than 1 dm? _____ **B.** Is 5 dm longer than 1 m? _____

C. Is 900 m longer than 1 km? _____ **D.** Is 1 m longer than 90 cm? _____

E. Is 1 m longer than 1 dm? _____ **F.** Is 20 cm longer than 1 m? _____

G. Is 5 mm longer than 1 cm? _____ **H.** Is 2 km longer than 1,500 m? _____

I. Is 2 cm longer than 10 mm? _____ **J.** Is 15 dm longer than 1 m? _____

Silent Letter in "kn"

Read each riddle. Write the **kn** word from the word list that answers the riddle.

knee	knife	knot	knapsack	knight	knoll	knocker

1. I can be found on a door. You use me to let someone know you are at the door. What am I? _____

2. You can put things inside of me and carry me. What am I? _____

3. I helped protect the king. I wore armor. Who am I? _____

4. I am part of your body. You can find me on your leg. What am I? _____

5. You must be careful with me. I help cut your food. What am I? _____

6. I am a small, round hill. What am I? _____

7. You can tie me in a piece of string. What am I? _____

Silent Letter in "wr"

Write the letters **wr** in front of each set of letters. Say the words.

1. _____inkle 2. _____eath 3. _____ong 4. _____angle

5. _____apper 6. _____eck 7. _____estle 8. _____ap

Say each **wr** word. Circle the picture of the word.

9. wrap 10. wrist 11. write 12. wring

Customary Length

Using an inch ruler, measure each line segment to the nearest inch.
Write the answer in the box to the right of the segment.

A. _____

B. _____

C. _____

D. _____

E. _____

F. _____

Customary Capacity

Rules:
- 2 cups = 1 pint
- 2 pints = 1 quart
- 4 quarts = 1 gallon

Example:
Is one cup greater than, less than, or equal to 1 pint?
If 2 cups = 1 pint
then 1 cup is <u>less than</u> 1 pint.

Complete each sentence using **more than**, **less than**, or **equal to**.
Write your answer on the line.

A. 2 pints are _____ 1 quart.

B. 1 pint is _____ 1 quart.

C. 3 quarts are _____ 1 gallon.

D. 3 cups are _____ 1 quart.

E. 1 gallon is _____ 1 pint.

F. 6 pints are _____ 3 quarts.

G. 2 pints are _____ 4 cups.

H. 8 quarts are _____ 2 gallons.

Silent Letter in "ck"

Read the words. Circle each word that ends with the letters **ck**.

1. jazz **2.** speech **3.** mask **4.** crutch

5. rock **6.** stick **7.** click **8.** lock

9. lake **10.** quack **11.** quick **12.** sick

Read each word group. Write the **ck** word from the word list that belongs with the group.

Word List sock stick neck quick rock truck

13. fast, speedy, _____

14. log, twig, _____

15. shoulder, arm, _____

16. stone, pebble, _____

17. shoe, feet, _____

18. car, motorcycle, _____

Silent Letter in "mb"

Say the name of each picture. Fill in the circle
next to the **mb** word that names the picture.

1. ⭕ thumb
 ⭕ dumb

2. ⭕ climb
 ⭕ tomb

3. ⭕ lamb
 ⭕ limb

Read each **mb** word. Write a sentence using the word.
Circle the letters **mb** .

4. lamb _____

5. numb _____

6. crumb _____

7. climb _____

8. comb _____

Area

Area is the space inside a figure. It is measured in **square units**.
You can find the area by adding the number of squares in the figure.

Look at the following figures and find the area of each.

A.

Area = _____ square units

B.

Area = _____ square units

Math

Reading a Map Grid

Sometimes a map is drawn with a **grid**. The number coordinates on the map grid below are located on both sides of the map. The letter coordinates are located at the top and bottom of the map.

Look at the locations of the different cities. Write the name of each city on the line beside the matching coordinates at the bottom of the page.

D-1 _____

C-2 _____

A-2 _____

B-3 _____

B-1 _____

E-4 _____

Area and Perimeter

Rules:

Area (A) is the number of square units inside a figure. To find the area of rectangles and squares, multiply the length times the width.

Perimeter (P) is the number of units around a figure. To find the perimeter of rectangles and squares, add the length of all four sides.

Examples:

A = 4 x 3 = 12 square units
P = 4 + 3 + 4 + 3 = 14 units

A.

Area = _____

Perimeter = _____

B.

Area = _____

Perimeter = _____

C.

Area = _____

Perimeter = _____

D.

Area = _____

Perimeter = _____

E.

Area = _____

Perimeter = _____

F.

Area = _____

Perimeter = _____

G.

Area = _____

Perimeter = _____

H.

Area = _____

Perimeter = _____

Outcomes

An **outcome** is the result of an event.

Decide whether the following outcomes are **certain** (will definitely happen), **possible** (might happen), or **impossible** (will not happen). Write your answer on the line.

1. It will rain tomorrow. _____

2. You will grow to be 50 feet tall. _____

3. The Vikings will win the Super Bowl next season. _____

4. Tomorrow will be 24 hours long. _____

5. Humans will travel to Mars. _____

6. New Year's Eve will fall on December 31st. _____

Homophones

Homophones are words that sound alike but are spelled differently and have different meanings.

Example: tail – tale

Circle the two words in each row that are homophones.

1.	bear	seen	saw	bare
2.	violet	vase	vain	vein
3.	drop	dew	down	due
4.	tee	tell	told	tea
5.	well	weight	wait	went
6.	him	hair	hare	held

Reading a Map

Marcia lives in Flower City. She has a new friend named Tina. Marcia invited Tina to her house for a visit. Marcia drew a map to help Tina find her house.

Look at the map and use it to answer the questions below.

1. The road where Marcia lives is _____.

2. The lane where Tina lives is _____.

3. What four roads cross the railroad tracks? _____

 _____.

4. What road intersects both Daffodil Road and Violet Road?

 _____.

5. How can you get across Bubbling Creek? _____

 _____.

6. What roads intersect Zinnia Street? _____

Punctuation

Place the correct punctuation mark at the end of each sentence in the story below. Write an ending to the story.

Making Pancakes

My sister and I woke early last Saturday morning We decided to make breakfast for Mom We took out the pancake mix We put the mix in a big bowl . We added eggs and milk I was stirring the batter My sister was pouring orange juice Then, the cat jumped onto the counter He tipped over the glass of juice and knocked the bowl to the floor Batter and juice went everywhere Next . . .

Understanding What I Read

Read the story. Then, answer the questions.

Nightly Navigator

Many people do not realize what bats do for us. They are some of our best nighttime insect exterminators. Over 900 kinds of bats exist in the world today. These bats can be anywhere from one-half inch long to over 15 inches long. Although most bats eat just insects, some dine on fruit and the nectar of flowers. As the only flying mammals on earth, bats should be recognized for their contributions to humans. Aside from controlling the insect population, bats are the main pollinators and seed spreaders for many tropical trees like mangoes, guavas, cashews, cloves, and Brazil nuts. Bats use their sonar-guided mouths and ears to enjoy a nightly dinner of millions of mosquitoes, mayflies, and moths.

1. What is the main idea of this paragraph?

 _____ .

2. How many different kinds of bats are there in the world?

 _____ .

3. What do bats like to eat?

 _____ .

4. How large can some species of bats get?

 _____ .

5. What kinds of tropical trees depend on the bat for spreading their seeds and for pollination?

 _____ .

Addressing Envelopes

Address the envelopes below using the information given.

The sender is:

Dr. James Madison
38 Carlton Place
Salem, NC 29532

The receiver is:

Ms. Mary Morton
149 Sparrow Street
Tucson, AZ 52974

The sender is:

Mrs. Alice Watson
9 Flag Avenue
Port Huron, MI 48060

The receiver is:

Miss Susan Coats
183 Spring Street
Denver, CO 50738

Answer Key

Short and Long Vowels Review

Read each sentence. Listen to the first vowel in the highlighted word.
Write ⁻ or ˘ over the vowel and circle the correct word after the sentence.

1. Ray skied down the **slōpe**. **(long)** short
2. I put my picture inside a **frāme**. **(long)** short
3. The **kīte** was flying high in the air. **(long)** short
4. I asked Sean to **tŏss** the ball to me. long **(short)**
5. Ann picked a **bŭnch** of flowers from the field. long **(short)**
6. Tina is Marie's **sĭster**. long **(short)**
7. Put those papers in the **trăsh**. long **(short)**
8. I sat on the **bĕnch** in the park. long **(short)**
9. The **tūbe** of toothpaste was empty. **(long)** short
10. Put **thōse** books on the shelf. **(long)** short
11. I need to get out of the sun and sit in the **shāde**. **(long)** short
12. Lisa wore a white **drĕss** to the party. long **(short)**

Number Patterns

Study each sequence of numbers.
Circle the group of numbers that continues the pattern.

A. 1, 3, 5, 7, 9, . . .
 10, 11, 12, 13 **(11, 13, 15, 17)** 12, 14, 16, 18
B. 3, 6, 9, 12, 15, . . .
 (18, 21, 24, 27) 16, 17, 18, 19 30, 60, 90, 120
C. 1, 4, 7, 10, . . .
 12, 14, 16, 18 11, 12, 13, 14 **(13, 16, 19, 22)**
D. 1, 7, 13, 19, . . .
 21, 28, 34, 40 **(25, 31, 37, 43)** 21, 23, 25, 27

16

Ordering Numbers

Rewrite the numbers in each row in order from **least** to **greatest**.

A. 6,283 683 561 656 561 656 683 6,283
B. 8,899 882 8,311 411 411 882 8,311 8,899

Rewrite the numbers in each row in order from **greatest** to **least**.

C. 737 3,778 7,138 347 7,138 3,778 737 347
D. 998 899 9,989 9,998 9,998 9,989 998 899

Long and Short Vowels Assessment

For each word, write ⁻ or ˘ over the vowel that
correctly completes the word. Write the letter on the line.

1. wr**ĕ**ck e̲ u 5. tr**ă**sh a̲ e 9. r**ū**le u̲ a
2. spr**ŭ**ng u̲ e 6. ch**ī**me e i̲ 10. bl**ā**ze a̲ e
3. h**ō**me o̲ e 7. sc**ō**pe o̲ e 11. c**ŏ**mmon o̲ a
4. f**ĭ**lm a i̲ 8. s**ī**ze e i̲ 12. t**ū**be u̲ a

BONUS
Divide a sheet of paper into two columns. Write the long vowel words from
above in one column and the short vowel words in the other column.

17

Addition Facts to 18

Add to solve the problems in the problem list. Then, find the
same problems in the puzzle. Circle the hidden problems and write
+ and = in the correct places. Problems are hidden across and down.

8 + 7 = 15	9 + 5 = 14	9 + 2 = 11	7 + 3 = 10	4 + 6 = 10	
6 + 7 = 13	7 + 6 = 13	9 + 9 = 18	4 + 7 = 11	6 + 8 = 14	
7 + 4 = 11	5 + 9 = 14	8 + 8 = 16	6 + 5 = 11	2 + 8 = 10	
9 + 8 = 17				6 + 7 = 13	
4 + 8 = 12				6 + 6 = 12	

18

Silent e

A **silent e** at the end of a word makes the first vowel have a long sound.
Say the words and listen to the vowel sounds.

glāz̶e̶ thēs̶e̶ shīn̶e̶ tōt̶e̶ fūm̶e̶

Read each word and circle the long vowel sound. Underline the silent e.

1. dōz̶e̶
2. brāv̶e̶
3. wīp̶e̶
4. pōk̶e̶
5. thrīv̶e̶
6. lōt̶e̶
7. trād̶e̶
8. rūl̶e̶
9. tōn̶e̶
10. jōk̶e̶
11. mād̶e̶
12. fīl̶e̶
13. twīc̶e̶
14. gām̶e̶
15. thēs̶e̶
16. stōv̶e̶
17. bōn̶e̶
18. blām̶e̶
19. whāl̶e̶
20. kīt̶e̶
21. māt̶e̶

Expanded Notation

Look at the key and the model for a three-digit number.
Then, fill in the missing information below.

Key
0 = hundreds
/ = tens
• = ones

Standard number: 482
Expanded notation: 400 + 80 + 2
Pictorial model: 0000 ///////// ••

	Standard number	Expanded notation	Pictorial model
A.	327	300 + 20 + 7	000 // •••••••
B.	254	200 + 50 + 4	00 ///// ••••
C.	845	800 + 40 + 5	00000000 //// •••••

19

Fiction or Nonfiction?

Stories can be divided into two different types. **Fiction** is drawn from the imagination, and the events and characters are not real. **Nonfiction** has only facts about people, places, subjects, and events that are real.

Read the following paragraph and write **fiction** or **nonfiction** in the box.

Army ants are some of the most feared types of ants. These are very destructive and can eat all living things in their paths. Army ants travel at night in groups of hundreds of thousands through the tropical forests of Africa and South America.

nonfiction

Now write your own story. On the bottom blank line, write whether your story is **fiction** or **nonfiction**.

Try to think of a story character you would like to be. Draw a picture of yourself as this new character.

Answers will vary. Pictures will vary.

20

Subtraction Facts to 18

Subtract to solve the problems in the problem lists. Then, find the same problems in the puzzle. Circle each problem and write − and = in the correct places. Problems are hidden across and down.

Problem List
11 − 5 = 6
13 − 5 = 8
12 − 7 = 5
11 − 8 = 3
16 − 7 = 9
10 − 8 = 2
11 − 8 = 3
5 − 0 = 5

Problem List
10 − 2 = 8
12 − 8 = 4
11 − 4 = 7
10 − 7 = 3
4 − 2 = 2
6 − 4 = 2
13 − 8 = 5
12 − 9 = 3

21

Number Sentences

Read each word problem.
Circle the number sentence that shows the correct answer.

A. Brian solved two difficult math problems. It took him 11 minutes to complete the first problem and 13 minutes to complete the second. How long did it take him to complete both problems?
 11 + 2 = 13 **(11 + 13 = 24)** 13 − 11 = 2 11 + 2 = 13

B. Mary invited 25 friends to her birthday party, but only 17 showed up. How many of the invited friends did not come?
 17 + 25 = 43 43 − 25 = 17 **(25 − 17 = 8)** 17 − 8 = 9

C. Sharon has already read 12 pages in her science book this evening. If she has to read 18 more pages tonight, how many pages was her reading assignment for tonight?
 12 + 6 = 18 **(18 + 12 = 30)** 30 + 12 = 42 18 − 6 = 12

Y as a Vowel

The letter **y** at the end of a word can make the
long e sound or the **long i** sound.

Write each word from the word list in the correct column.

Word List
hurry
spy
fry
party
by
busy
lazy
try

1. y = ē sound	2. y = ī sound
hurry	spy
party	fry
busy	by
lazy	try

22

Schwa Sound (ə)

Some vowels do not make a long or short sound.
These vowels make the **schwa** sound.
The symbol **ə** means a vowel makes a schwa sound.

Say the words. Listen to the schwa sound (ə) in each.

sofa (sofə) lemon (leman) father (fathər)

For each pair of words, underline the schwa symbol in the first word.
Circle the word that makes the schwa sound in the second word.

1. system syst**ə**m 2. circas circ**ə**s 3. about **(ə)**bout
4. forward forw**ə**d 5. roben rob**ə**n 6. apren **(ə)**pron
7. choras chor**ə**s 8. camera camer**ə** 9. pencal penc**(ə)**l
10. letter lett**ə**r 11. over ov**ə**r 12. campar camp**(ə)**r

Story Problems

Read each word problem and circle the correct answer.
Use extra paper to help solve the problems if you need it.

A. Marcia will run every day next week. If she runs 1 mile on Sunday, 3 miles on Monday, and 5 miles on Tuesday, how many miles will she run on Wednesday?
 9 11 **(7)** 13

B. John and Tonya went to the store to buy 2 boxes of oatmeal cookies. Each box has 12 cookies. How many cookies will John and Tonya have?
 (24) 36 48 16

C. Alex has 23 marbles. If Alex has 4 friends and he gives each friend a marble, how many marbles will Alex have left?
 27 **(19)** 4 20

23

Reading and Writing Numbers

A number is usually written using digits in the appropriate place value spots. This is called **standard form**.

Examples: five thousand, two hundred fifty-one = **5,251**
twenty-two thousand, thirty-three = **22,033**

Write each number in standard form on the line.

A. six hundred thirty-four = 634
B. eight thousand, two hundred fifty-one = 8,251
C. nine thousand, three hundred twenty-two = 9,322
D. twenty-seven thousand, eight hundred = 27,800
E. seventy thousand, one hundred two = 70,102
F. eighty-three thousand, three hundred eleven = 83,311

Beginning Blends: bl, cl, fl

Write each word in the correct column.

flute blue clean clasp float fleet blimp blink cloak

bl	cl	fl
blue	clean	flute
blimp	clasp	float
blink	cloak	fleet

24

Answer Key

Expanded Notation

Math

Expanded notation is writing a number to show the value of each digit in the number. **Examples:** 583 = **500 + 80 + 3**
six hundred fifty-two = **600 + 50 + 2**

Circle the letter beside the correct expanded notation for each number.

Eight hundred seventy-five =

A. 8,000 + 70 + 5
B. 800 + 70 + 5
C. 80,000 + 700 + 50
D. 800,000 + 70 + 5

Six thousand forty-eight =

A. 6,000 + 400 + 80
B. 10,000 + 6,000 + 400 + 80
C. 6,000 + 40 + 8
D. 60,000 + 40 + 8

Beginning Blends: gl, pl, sl

Phonics

Say the word that names each picture.
Circle the beginning blend of each word.

1. gl / pl / sl
2. gl / pl / sl
3. gl / pl / sl
4. gl / pl / sl
5. gl / pl / sl
6. gl / pl / sl

25

Nouns

Language Arts

Common nouns name any one of a group of things.
Proper nouns name a specific person, place, or thing.

Each sentence has one common noun and one proper noun. Write the common noun to the left of the sentence and the proper noun to the right.

Common Nouns		Proper Nouns
cousin	My cousin lives in Spain.	Spain
bear	Smokey is a famous bear.	Smokey
family	My family ate at Pizza Barn.	Pizza Barn
city	Ogden is a beautiful city.	Ogden
scientist	Isaac Newton was a scientist.	Isaac Newton
satellite	The first satellite was Sputnik I.	Sputnik I
camera	George Eastman made cameras.	George Eastman
months	The Pilgrims sailed for two months.	Pilgrims

Comparing Numbers

Math

Study the examples below. To compare each pair of numbers, use less than (<), greater than (>), or equal to (=). Write the correct symbol in each oval.

Examples: 375 (<) 6,200 7,000 (=) 7,000 3,482 (>) 2,843

A. 620 (<) 6,200
B. 493 (>) 439
C. 6,432 (<) 16,408
D. 9,286 (<) 13,489
E. 724 (=) 724
F. 3,080 (<) 3,800
G. 45,015 (<) 45,016
H. 397,124 (<) 387,425
I. 488,188 (>) 488,018

26

Two-Digit Addition with Regrouping

Math

Add to solve the problems.

A.	54 + 26 = 80	B.	44 + 39 = 83	C.	19 + 76 = 95
D.	24 + 47 = 71	E.	38 + 57 = 95	F.	29 + 64 = 93
G.	49 + 31 = 80	H.	78 + 12 = 90	I.	36 + 46 = 82

Beginning Blends: br, cr, dr, fr

Phonics

Say the name of each picture. Fill in the circle if the word begins with the blend in the box.

1. dr ●
2. cr ●
3. br ●
4. fr ●
5. cr ●
6. br ●
7. cr
8. br ●
9. fr ●
10. dr ●
11. fr
12. dr ●

27

Beginning Blends: gr, pr, tr

Phonics

Say the names of the pictures.
Circle the picture that begins with each blend shown.

1. gr
2. pr
3. tr

Read each word. Circle the beginning blend gr, pr, or tr in each word.

4. preview
5. produce
6. truly
7. triumph
8. tread
9. prop
10. tree
11. predict
12. grew
13. ground
14. gruel
15. giant

Two-Digit Subtraction with Regrouping

Math

Subtract to solve the problems.

A.	70 - 19 = 51	B.	82 - 17 = 65	C.	70 - 22 = 48	D.	90 - 79 = 11
E.	78 - 59 = 19	F.	53 - 14 = 39	G.	66 - 8 = 58	H.	54 - 38 = 16

28

Pronouns

Language Arts

Circle the pronoun that completes each sentence.

1. _____ grew corn and tomatoes in his garden.
 Him / His / **He**

2. Please tell _____ what vegetables you would like to plant this year.
 we / mine / **us**

3. Tisha and _____ love to plant our watermelon seeds.
 we / **I** / us

4. Mother wants to plant flowers in her garden so that _____ will have something special.
 us / mine / **she**

5. We plant carrots, lettuce, and beans because _____ are good to eat.
 they / them / she

Addition with Regrouping

Math

A.	35 + 27 = 62	B.	85 + 56 = 141	C.	28 + 14 = 42	D.	78 + 66 = 144
E.	348 + 235 = 583	F.	628 + 597 = 1,225	G.	565 + 217 = 782	H.	4,188 + 176 = 4,364

29

Adding Two or More Addends

Math

Keep the place values lined up to find the right sum. Solve the problems.

A.	62 + 27 + 89 = 89	D.	736 + 89 + 104 = 929	G.	6,428 + 1,375 + 3,684 = 11,487	J.	5,894 + 1,388 + 3,137 = 10,419
B.	75 + 85 = 160	E.	3,482 + 437 + 68 = 3,987	H.	30,147 + 25,236 + 42,613 = 97,996	K.	28,123 + 33,294 + 46,510 = 107,927
C.	54 + 92 = 146	F.	246 + 442 + 53 = 741	I.	2,804 + 1,366 + 5,391 = 9,561	L.	14,738 + 22,856 + 17,979 = 55,573

Beginning Blends: sk, sm, sn, sp

Phonics

Say the name of each picture. Circle the word that names the picture and write its beginning blend.

1. smell / spoon / skill — sp
2. smoke / spy / snack — sm
3. skunk / snowman / snare — sn
4. smear / spore / skate — sk
5. smack / skirt / sniff — sk
6. spool / skit / snoop — sp
7. smile / sneak / spoot — sm
8. skull / spill / snail — sn

30

Action Verbs

Grammar

An **action verb** tells what the subject of a sentence does.
Look at the action verbs in the following sentences.

Dino **plays** football in the fall. We **walk** home every day.

Underline the action verb in each sentence.

1. Small airplanes **fly** over our house every afternoon at 5:00.
2. The rooster on our farm **crows** every morning at 6:00.
3. My dad **plows** the fields near our house in the spring.
4. The ducks in the pond **splash** water everywhere each afternoon.
5. Mother **feeds** the chickens twice a day.
6. My brother and I **clean** the barn every Saturday.

Two-Digit Subtraction

Math

Subtract to solve the problems.

A.	17 - 16 = 11	B.	46 - 25 = 21	C.	84 - 53 = 31	D.	78 - 16 = 62
E.	25 - 14 = 11	F.	27 - 13 = 14	G.	75 - 31 = 44	H.	68 - 14 = 14
I.	23 - 12 = 11	J.	42 - 31 = 11	K.	24 - 13 = 11	L.	82 - 71 = 11

31

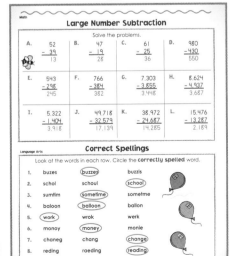

Large Number Subtraction

Math

Solve the problems.

A.	52 - 39 = 13	B.	47 - 19 = 28	C.	61 - 25 = 36	D.	980 - 430 = 550
E.	543 - 298 = 245	F.	766 - 384 = 382	G.	7,303 - 3,855 = 3,448	H.	8,624 - 4,937 = 3,687
I.	5,322 - 1,404 = 3,918	J.	49,718 - 32,579 = 17,139	K.	38,972 - 24,687 = 14,285	L.	15,476 - 13,287 = 2,189

Correct Spellings

Language Arts

Look at the words in each row. Circle the **correctly spelled** word.

1. buzes / **buzzes** / buzzis
2. schol / schoul / **school**
3. sumfim / **sometime** / sometme
4. baloon / **balloon** / ballon
5. **work** / wrok / werk
6. monoy / **money** / monie
7. chaneg / chang / **change**
8. reding / raeding / **reading**
9. **homework** / homwork / homewrok

32

Syllables

Grammar

Answer the questions. Write the answers on the lines.

hip•po•pot•a•mus star•fish en•cy•clo•pe•di•a
ta•ran•tu•la zuc•chi•ni

1. Which word has five syllables? **hippopotamus**
2. How many syllables does **encyclopedia** have? **6**
3. Which word has three syllables? **zucchini**
4. How many syllables does **starfish** have? **2**
5. Which word has one syllable? **newt**
6. How many syllables does **tarantula** have? **4**

Multiplication Facts for 0

Math

When the number 0 is a factor, the product is always 0.

3 × 0 = 0 0 × 9 = 0

Complete the facts for 0.

0 × 0 = **0** 0 × 5 = **0**
0 × 1 = **0** 0 × 6 = **0**
0 × 2 = **0** 0 × 7 = **0**
0 × 3 = **0** 0 × 8 = **0**
0 × 4 = **0** 0 × 9 = **0**

35

Answer Key

Pictograph

The following **pictograph** shows the favorite pets of students in Mrs. Mill's third grade class. Each picture stands for one student's vote.

Favorite Pets

Number of Votes — Iguanas, Snakes, Gerbils, Cats, Dogs

Look at the graph and answer the questions.

A. How many children voted for gerbils? __4__

B. What pet received the fewest votes? __iguanas__

C. How many more votes did cats receive than snakes? __3__

D. How many children voted in all? __20__

E. Which two pets were equally popular? __cats__ __dogs__

36

Multiplication Facts for 1

When the number **1** is a factor, the product equals the other factor.

1 × 9 = 9 2 × 1 = 2

Complete the facts for 1.

1 × 0 = __0__ 1 × 5 = __5__
1 × 1 = __1__ 1 × 6 = __6__
1 × 2 = __2__ 1 × 7 = __7__
1 × 3 = __3__ 1 × 8 = __8__
1 × 4 = __4__ 1 × 9 = __9__

Beginning Blends: st, sw, tw

Say each word below. If the word begins with the **st** blend, circle it. If the word begins with the **sw** blend, draw an **X** on it. If the word begins with the **tw** blend, underline it.

1. twelve 2. (staple) 3. twist 4. tweak 5. swan 6. (stand)
7. swift 8. swipe 9. (sting) 10. sweep 11. twilight 12. (stare)

Say the name of each picture. Write the two letters that make up the word's beginning blend.

13. st 14. st 15. sw 16. tw 17. sw 18. sw

37

Beginning Blends: scr, spl, spr, str

Circle the **beginning blend** in each word below.

1. scratch 2. stride 3. sprinkle 4. spruce 5. splay
6. sprig 7. split 8. scribble 9. straight 10. street
11. splurge 12. scroll 13. stream 14. spray 15. sprig

Use the beginning blend **scr, spl, spr,** or **str** to complete the name of each picture.

16. scr ub 17. spl inter 18. spr ing 19. scr eam 20. str oller 21. spr inkler

Multiplication Facts for 2

Multiply to solve the problems.

A. 3 × 2 = 6 B. 8 × 2 = 16 C. 0 × 2 = 0 D. 2 × 6 = 12
E. 5 × 2 = 10 F. 2 × 7 = 14 G. 4 × 2 = 8 H. 2 × 2 = 4
I. 2 × 9 = 18 J. 1 × 2 = 2 K. 2 × 8 = 16 L. 2 × 5 = 10

38

Story Webs

Complete the story web. Use the words in the web to write a story. Be sure to use capital letters and periods. Think of a *cool* title for your story.

Things to Think About

Who is this story about?
Where does this story take place?
How does this story begin?
What happens next?
How will this story end?

cactus hot
camel desert

Stories will vary.

39

Multiplication Facts for 3

Use the sets below to help complete the multiplication facts.

A. 1 × 3 = __3__ B. 9 × 3 = __27__ C. 4 × 3 = __12__
D. 5 × 3 = __15__ E. 6 × 3 = __18__ F. 2 × 3 = __6__
G. 3 × 3 = __9__ H. 7 × 3 = __21__ I. 8 × 3 = __24__
J. 0 × 3 = __0__ K. 3 × 9 = __27__ L. 3 × 3 = __9__

Vowel Sound ai/ay

Write a word from the word list under each picture.

Word List waist ray crayon paint hay train

1. ray 2. paint 3. hay
4. crayon 5. waist 6. train

40

Word Searches

Parties!

Word List: party, celebrate, birthday, decorate, special, excited, surprise, invite, ribbon, balloon

Circle the words from the word list in the puzzle below.

41

Success!

Word List: deed, spotlight, admire, special, student, success, achieve, ribbon, effort, award

Circle the words from the word list in the puzzle below.

Sports

Word List: sports, compete, field, referee, game, player, uniform, mascot, champion, overtime

Circle the words from the word list in the puzzle below.

42

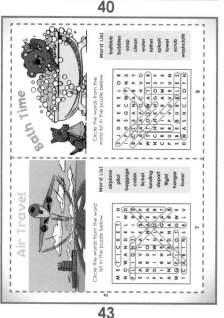

Bath Time

Word List: bathtub, bubbles, soap, clean, water, lather, splash, towel, scrub, washcloth

Circle the words from the word list in the puzzle below.

Air Travel

Word List: airplane, pilot, baggage, cabin, ticket, landing, depart, flight, hangar, tower

Circle the words from the word list in the puzzle below.

43

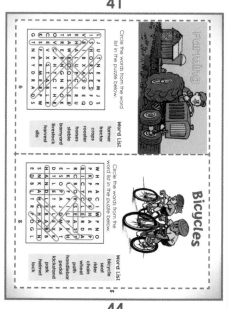

Farming

Word List: farmer, tractor, crops, rooster, horses, stable, barnyard, livestock, harvest, silo

Circle the words from the word list in the puzzle below.

Bicycles

Word List: bicycle, rider, wheel, chain, path, pedal, handlebar, helmet, kickstand, lock, seat

Circle the words from the word list in the puzzle below.

44

Answer Key

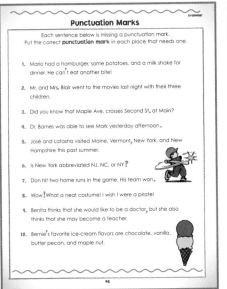

Punctuation Marks

Each sentence below is missing a punctuation mark.
Put the correct **punctuation mark** in each place that needs one.

1. Mario had a hamburger, some potatoes, and a milk shake for dinner. He can't eat another bite!

2. Mr. and Mrs. Blair went to the movies last night with their three children.

3. Did you know that Maple Ave. crosses Second St. at Main?

4. Dr. Barnes was able to see Mark yesterday afternoon.

5. José and Latasha visited Maine, Vermont, New York, and New Hampshire this past summer.

6. Is New York abbreviated NJ, NC, or NY?

7. Don hit two home runs in the game. His team won.

8. Wow! What a neat costume! I wish I were a pirate!

9. Benita thinks that she would like to be a doctor, but she also thinks that she may become a teacher.

10. Bernie's favorite ice-cream flavors are chocolate, vanilla, butter pecan, and maple nut.

45

45

Vowel Sound ee/ea

Complete each word by writing the letters **ee** or **ea** on the line.

1. wh _ee_ l
2. ind _ee_ d
3. cl _ea_ n
4. l _ea_ ve
5. sp _ea_ k
6. sn _ee_ ze
7. tr _ea_ t
8. sl _ee_ p
9. s _ee_ n
10. b _ee_ p
11. sl _ee_ t
12. tr _ee_
13. dr _ea_ m
14. str _ee_ t
15. gr _ea_ se

BONUS Write **ee** or **ea** to make each word match the clue.

st _ee_ l (hard metal) p _ee_ k (to look) w _ea_ k (not strong)

Multiplication Facts for 4

When a number is multiplied by 4, it is the same as adding the number to itself 4 times.

$4 \times 3 = 12$ is the same as $3 + 3 + 3 + 3 = 12$

Complete the facts for 4.

$4 \times 0 = 0$ $4 \times 5 = 20$
$4 \times 1 = 4$ $4 \times 6 = 24$
$4 \times 2 = 8$ $4 \times 7 = 28$
$4 \times 3 = 12$ $4 \times 8 = 32$
$4 \times 4 = 16$ $4 \times 9 = 36$

46

46

Multiplication Facts for 5

Use the sets of 5 below to help complete the multiplication facts.

A. $4 \times 5 = 20$ B. $4 \times 5 = 20$ C. $8 \times 5 = 40$
D. $7 \times 5 = 35$ E. $2 \times 5 = 10$ F. $9 \times 5 = 45$
G. $3 \times 5 = 15$ H. $6 \times 5 = 30$ I. $1 \times 5 = 5$

Vowel Sound oa

Use the words from the word list to complete each sentence.
Circle the **long o** sound of **oa** in each word.

Word List: loan, afloat, coach, oak, toaster, coast

1. Mr. Collins is our basketball **coach**.
2. The acorns fell from the **oak** tree.
3. We hoped our raft would stay **afloat** in the water.
4. The storm hit the Florida **coast** last night.
5. Mindy asked if I would **loan** her my bike.
6. Put the bread in the **toaster**, then butter it.

Complete each word by writing the letters **oa**.
Read the word and listen for the **long o** sound.

7. r _oa_ d
8. c _oa_ l
9. t _oa_ d
10. g _oa_ t
11. l _oa_ d
12. b _oa_ t
13. s _oa_ p
14. g _oa_ l
15. _oa_ ts

47

47

Vowel Sound ue/ui

Complete each word by writing **ue** or **ui** on the line.
Read the words and listen for the **long u** sound.

1. s _ui_ t
2. cr _ue_ l
3. s _ue_
4. fr _ui_ t
5. br _ui_ se
6. f _ue_ l
7. tr _ue_
8. d _ue_ l
9. d _ue_ l
10. n _ui_ sance
11. cr _ui_ se
12. j _ui_ ce
13. cl _ue_
14. gl _ue_
15. T _ue_ sday

Logical Thinking

Read the following word problems. Make notes to help you find the order of the people in each problem. Circle the correct answer.

A. Four marathon runners ran in a race. Use the clues to determine the winner.

Mario ran faster than Shane.
Shane ran faster than Randy.
Tyler ran faster than Mario.

Who won the race?
a. Mario c. Shane
b. Randy d. Tyler ✓

B. Davis lined up his four sisters by height. Use the clues below to determine the order of the sisters.

Sally is taller than Kendra.
Mary is the tallest sister.
Trisha is not as tall as Kendra.

In what order did the sisters stand?
a. Mary, Trisha, Kendra, Sally
b. Mary, Sally, Trisha, Kendra
c. Mary, Sally, Kendra, Trisha ✓
d. Sally, Mary, Trisha, Kendra

48

48

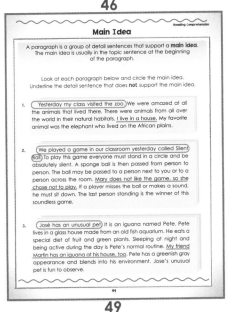

Main Idea

A paragraph is a group of detail sentences that support a **main idea**. The main idea is usually in the topic sentence at the beginning of the paragraph.

Look at each paragraph below and circle the main idea. Underline the detail sentence that does **not** support the main idea.

1. (Yesterday my class visited the zoo.) We were amazed at all the animals that lived there. There were animals from all over the world in their natural habitats. I live in a house. My favorite animal was the elephant who lived on the African plains.

2. (We played a game in our classroom yesterday called Silent Ball.) To play this game everyone must stand in a circle and be absolutely silent. A sponge ball is then passed from person to person. The ball may be passed to a person next to you or to a person across the room. Mary does not like the game, so she chose not to play. If a player misses the ball or makes a sound, he must sit down. The last person standing is the winner of this soundless game.

3. (José has an unusual pet.) It is an iguana named Pete. Pete lives in a glass house made from an old fish aquarium. He eats a special diet of fruit and green plants. Sleeping at night and being active during the day is Pete's normal routine. My friend Martin has an iguana at his house, too. Pete has a greenish gray appearance and blends into his environment. Jose's unusual pet is fun to observe.

49

49

Beat the Clock (Multiplication Facts to 5)

Time: _____ Number correct: _____

50

50

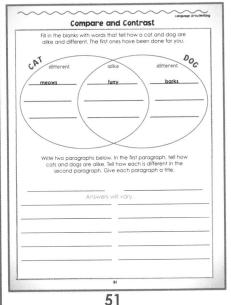

Compare and Contrast

Fill in the blanks with words that tell how a cat and dog are alike and different. The first ones have been done for you.

CAT — different — alike — different — DOG

meows / furry / barks

Write two paragraphs below. In the first paragraph, tell how cats and dogs are alike. Tell how each is different in the second paragraph. Give each paragraph a title.

Answers will vary.

51

51

Fractions

Fractions show parts of the whole.

Circle the correct fraction to answer each question.

A. What part of the drawing is shaded? $\frac{2}{5}$ $\frac{1}{4}$ $\frac{4}{5}$ ✓ $\frac{2}{3}$

B. What part of the drawing is shaded? $\frac{1}{3}$ $\frac{3}{4}$ ✓ $\frac{2}{4}$

C. Which fraction names the shaded part of the set? $\frac{3}{4}$ ✓ $\frac{2}{3}$ $\frac{3}{4}$

D. Which fraction names the shaded part of the set? $\frac{1}{2}$ $\frac{3}{4}$ ✓ $\frac{2}{3}$ $\frac{1}{3}$

Vowel Digraph oo

Compare the sound of the letters **oo** in the words **look** and **moon**. Read each word and circle the matching sound.

oo = look oo = moon

1. gloomy — moon
2. spooky — moon
3. crook — look
4. boot — moon
5. proof — moon
6. rooster — moon
7. book — look
8. foolish — moon
9. cook — look
10. wool — look
11. scoop — moon
12. took — look
13. stood — look
14. broom — moon
15. cookie — look

52

52

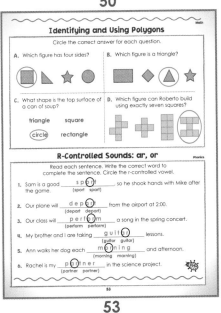

Identifying and Using Polygons

Circle the correct answer for each question.

A. Which figure has four sides? (square)
B. Which figure is a triangle? (triangle)
C. What shape is the top surface of a can of soup? triangle / square / (circle) / rectangle
D. Which figure can Roberto build using exactly seven squares?

R-Controlled Sounds: ar, or

Read each sentence. Write the correct word to complete the sentence. Circle the r-controlled vowel.

1. Sam is a good **sport**, so he shook hands with Mike after the game. (sport / sport)
2. Our plane will **depart** from the airport at 2:00. (depart / depart)
3. Our class will **perform** a song in the spring concert. (perform / perform)
4. My brother and I are taking **guitar** lessons. (guitar / guitar)
5. Ann walks her dog each **morning** and afternoon. (morning / morning)
6. Rachel is my **partner** in the science project. (partner / partner)

53

53

149

Answer Key

Symmetry

Math

Symmetry occurs when two halves of a figure match exactly when folded together. The line of symmetry is the location of the fold.

Example: This square shows a **line of symmetry** from top to bottom (vertical).

In each group, circle the figure that has a line of symmetry.

A. B. C.

R-Controlled Sounds: er, ir, ur

Phonics

Choose a word from the word list to complete each sentence.
Circle the letters that make the r-controlled vowel sound.

1. Please ____enter____ the room quietly.
2. I put the money in my mother's ____purse____.
3. Sally won ____first____ place ribbon in the race.
4. The ____nurse____ took my temperature.
5. We went to the movies ____after____ lunch.
6. The ballerina loved to ____dance____.

Word List
first
enter
after
nurse
twirl
purse

Circle the letters that make the r-controlled vowel sound in each word.

7. p e r f e c t
8. c u r b
9. r u b b e r
10. n u r s e
11. b r o t h e r
12. u r g e
13. h e r m i t
14. t u r t l e
15. w h i r l
16. c u r s e
17. c u r t a i n
18. p u r p l e

54

Multiplication Facts 0–5

Math

Multiply to solve the problems in the problem list.
Then, find the same problems in the puzzle. Circle the hidden problems and write x and = in the correct places. Problems are hidden across and down.

Problem List

1 x 4 =	4
5 x 3 =	15
0 x 3 =	0
4 x 4 =	16
2 x 4 =	8
5 x 5 =	25
3 x 3 =	9
0 x 1 =	0
4 x 5 =	20
2 x 2 =	4
1 x 1 =	1
5 x 2 =	10
3 x 2 =	6
4 x 1 =	4
4 x 3 =	12

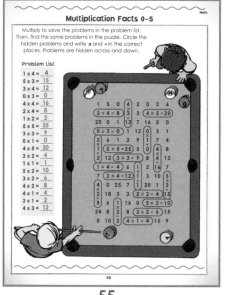

55

New Vocabulary Words

Use a dictionary to help you answer the questions below.
You will have fun learning some new words and interesting facts.
Look up the highlighted words and answer the questions on the lines.

1. Is a goldfinch a bag full of gold or a bird?
 ____a bird____
2. If you were on a jetty, would you be on a jet or a wall along a waterfront?
 ____a wall along a waterfront____
3. Is a yak a long-haired ox or a person that likes to talk?
 ____a long-haired ox____
4. Would you draw a parallelogram or do gymnastics on it?
 ____draw it____

Multiplication Facts for 6

Math

When a number is multiplied by 6, it is the same as adding the number to itself 6 times.

$6 \times 3 = 18$ is the same as $3 + 3 + 3 + 3 + 3 + 3 = 18$

Complete the facts for 6.

6 x 0 = __0__	6 x 5 = __30__
6 x 1 = __6__	6 x 6 = __36__
6 x 2 = __12__	6 x 7 = __42__
6 x 3 = __18__	6 x 8 = __48__
6 x 4 = __24__	6 x 9 = __54__

56

Understanding What I Read

Reading Comprehension

Read the story. Then, answer the questions.

The Wright Brothers

Orville and Wilbur Wright were famous American brothers. They owned a bicycle shop in Dayton, Ohio. Although they were interested in bicycles, they also loved the idea of flying. In 1896, they began to experiment, or try new ideas, with flight. They started by testing kites and then gliders, which are motorless planes. These tests taught them how an airplane should rise, turn, and come back to earth. The brothers made over 700 glider flights at Kitty Hawk, a field in North Carolina. This was fun but not good enough for them. Orville and Wilbur put a small engine on a plane they named Flyer I. On December 17, 1903, they took the first motor-powered flight that lasted about one minute. The brothers continued to experiment until they could stay in the air for over one hour.

1. What was the main idea of the story? Circle the correct answer.
 a. Testing new ideas is important.
 b. Flyer I was the first airplane.
 c. The Wright brothers were early pilots.
2. What does the word experiment mean? Circle the correct answer.
 a. to try new ideas
 b. to test kites
 c. to stay in the air for one hour
3. Where did the brothers test their gliders and plane? ____Kitty Hawk, North Carolina____
4. How long did their first motor-powered flight last? ____about one minute____
5. How did the brothers learn about what makes planes work? ____by experimenting____

57

Diphthong au

Phonics

Complete each sentence with a word from the word list.
Write the word and circle the au diphthong.

Word List

applause	vault	naughty
because	fault	caught

1. The ____applause____ was coming from the theater.
2. The bank teller got money from the ____vault____.
3. We ____caught____ ten fish on our fishing trip.
4. It was my ____fault____ that we were late for the movie.
5. The ____naughty____ puppy chewed up the shoe.
6. We did not have school yesterday ____because____ it was a holiday.

Multiplication Facts for 7

Math

Multiply to solve the problems.

A. 3 x 7 = 21
B. 1 x 7 = 7
C. 7 x 7 = 49
D. 8 x 7 = __56__
E. 7 x 9 = __63__
F. 2 x 7 = __14__
G. 7 x 6 = 42
H. 7 x 4 = 28
I. 7 x 5 = 35
J. 4 x 7 = __28__
K. 7 x 3 = __21__
L. 9 x 7 = __63__

58

Multiplication Facts for 8

Math

Multiply to solve the problems.

A. 4 x 8 = 32
B. 8 x 8 = 64
C. 6 x 8 = 48
D. 7 x 8 = __56__
E. 3 x 8 = __24__
F. 5 x 8 = __40__
G. 8 x 0 = 0
H. 8 x 1 = 8
I. 9 x 8 = 72

Diphthong aw

Phonics

Read each sentence. Write the correct word to complete the sentence.

1. We cut down the tree with a ____saw____. (saw sau)
2. The farmer put ____straw____ in the barn to keep the horses warm. (straw srau)
3. We stood under the ____awning____ so we would not get wet. (awning auning)
4. The little ____fawn____ could hardly walk. (faun fawn)
5. Put the meat on the counter to ____thaw____. (thaw thau)
6. We gazed in ____awe____ as the acrobat walked on the high wire. (aue awe)
7. My baby brother will ____crawl____ before he learns to walk. (craul crawl)

59

Grid Coordinates

Math

Look at the lines on the grid below. **Grid coordinates** are formed by the letters on the bottom and the numbers on the left side. If you look at the coordinates (C, 4), you should find the Enchanted Woods.

Story Town

Look at each fairy-tale place on the map and find its coordinates.
Write the coordinates for each place beside its name.

King's Castle	F	6	Gingerbread House	F, 3
Troll Bridge	A	2	Dragon's Cave	H, 1
Bear's House	H	5	Old Woman's Shoe	J, 2

60

Poetry—Haiku

Writing

Haiku is a form of Japanese poetry that follows a special pattern of 17 syllables. There are 5 syllables in the first line, 7 in the second line, and 5 in the third line. Most haiku poetry is about nature.

Read the following haiku poem.

Flakes of snow outside.
Icicles hanging from eaves.
Winter is here now.

Use the lines to write a Haiku poem of your own about apples, summer, or anything you want.

____Poems will vary.____

Comparing Fractions

Math

Write >, <, or = in the circle to make a true math statement.

A. $\frac{2}{3}$ > $\frac{1}{3}$
B. $\frac{12}{13}$ > $\frac{11}{13}$
C. $\frac{1}{12}$ < $\frac{1}{3}$
D. $\frac{5}{9}$ < $\frac{6}{9}$
E. $\frac{2}{6}$ < $\frac{3}{5}$
F. $\frac{2}{5}$ = $\frac{4}{10}$
G. $\frac{1}{4}$ = $\frac{2}{8}$
H. $\frac{3}{6}$ > $\frac{1}{4}$
I. $\frac{3}{8}$ < $\frac{5}{8}$

61

Multiplication Facts for 9

Math

Write the correct factor to complete each multiplication fact.

A. [4] x 9 = 36
B. 3 x [9] = 27
C. [2] x 9 = 18
D. [6] x 9 = 54
E. [5] x 9 = 45
F. [7] x 9 = 63
G. 1 x [9] = 9
H. 2 x [9] = 18
I. [0] x 9 = 0
J. [9] x 7 = 63
K. 9 x [1] = 9
L. 9 x [5] = 45

Alphabetical Order

Language Arts

Number the words in each group alphabetically from 1 to 5.
You will need to look all the way to the fourth or fifth letter in each group before you start numbering.

1. 3 peanut
 1 peacock
 4 pear
 2 peak
 5 peat

2. 2 greet
 1 greenhouse
 5 grew
 3 grenade
 4 gremlin

3. 2 alligator
 1 alley
 3 allow
 5 allude
 4 allspice

4. 1 iceberg
 4 icehouse
 2 icebox
 5 Iceland
 3 icebreaker

62

150

Answer Key

Singular and Plural Possessives
Grammar

Put an apostrophe in the correct position. Then, complete the sentence.

1. Several astronauts' spacesuits _____
2. That boy's football _____
3. The three poodles' fur _____
4. The four cats' claws _____
5. This week's laundry basket _____
6. My three friends' bikes _____ Sentences will vary.
7. The sun's rays _____
8. This robin's nest _____
9. The elf's voice _____
10. The two beavers' dams _____

Using Context Clues
Reading Comprehension

When you come to a word you don't know, use the **context clues**, or other words around it, to help you figure out the meaning.

Use context clues to figure out the meaning of each highlighted word below. Circle the correct meaning.

1. The green light coming from the haunted house was frightening. It was an **eerie** sight!
 a. green b. (spooky) c. funny

2. We must leave soon. We must **depart** as soon as everyone is ready.
 a. watch b. (leave) c. sign

3. The **clasp** of the seat belt was not fastened correctly.
 a. (buckle) b. strap c. seat

63

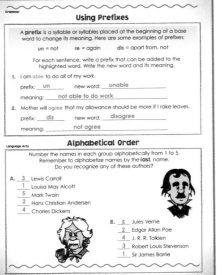

Using Prefixes
Grammar

A **prefix** is a syllable or syllables placed at the beginning of a base word to change its meaning. Here are some examples of prefixes:

un = not re = again dis = apart from, not

For each sentence, write a prefix that can be added to the highlighted word. Write the new word and its meaning.

1. I am **able** to do all of my work.
 prefix: un new word: unable
 meaning: not able to do work

2. Mother will **agree** that my allowance should be more if I rake leaves.
 prefix: dis new word: disagree
 meaning: not agree

Alphabetical Order
Language Arts

Number the names in each group alphabetically from 1 to 5. Remember to alphabetize names by the **last** name. Do you recognize any of these authors?

A.
3 Lewis Carroll
1 Louisa May Alcott
5 Mark Twain
2 Hans Christian Andersen
4 Charles Dickens

B.
5 Jules Verne
2 Edgar Allan Poe
4 J. R. R. Tolkien
3 Robert Louis Stevenson
1 Sir James Barrie

64

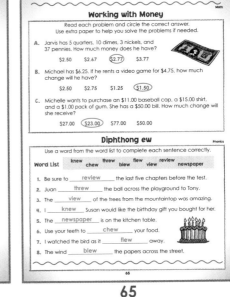

Working with Money
Math

Read each problem and circle the correct answer. Use extra paper to help you solve the problems if needed.

A. Jarvis has 5 quarters, 10 dimes, 3 nickels, and 37 pennies. How much money does he have?
 $2.50 $2.67 ($2.77) $3.77

B. Michael has $6.25. If he rents a video game for $4.75, how much change will he have?
 $2.50 $2.75 $1.25 ($1.50)

C. Michelle wants to purchase an $11.00 baseball cap, a $15.00 shirt, and a $1.00 pack of gum. She has a $50.00 bill. How much change will she receive?
 $27.00 ($23.00) $77.00 $50.00

Diphthong ew
Phonics

Use a word from the word list to complete each sentence correctly.

Word List: knew chew threw blew flew view review newspaper

1. Be sure to review the last five chapters before the test.
2. Juan threw the ball across the playground to Tony.
3. The view of the trees from the mountaintop was amazing.
4. I knew Susan would like the birthday gift you bought for her.
5. The newspaper is on the kitchen table.
6. Use your teeth to chew your food.
7. I watched the bird as it flew away.
8. The wind blew the papers across the street.

65

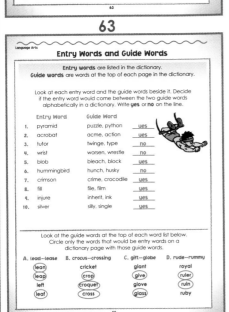

Entry Words and Guide Words
Language Arts

Entry words are listed in the dictionary.
Guide words are words at the top of each page in the dictionary.

Look at each entry word and the guide words beside it. Decide if the entry word would come between the two guide words alphabetically in a dictionary. Write **yes** or **no** on the line.

	Entry Word	Guide Word	
1.	pyramid	puzzle, python	yes
2.	acrobat	acme, action	yes
3.	tutor	twinge, type	no
4.	wrist	worsen, wrestle	no
5.	blob	bleach, block	yes
6.	hummingbird	hunch, husky	no
7.	crimson	crime, crocodile	yes
8.	fill	file, film	no
9.	injure	inherit, ink	yes
10.	silver	silly, single	yes

Look at the guide words at the top of each word list below. Circle only the words that would be entry words on a dictionary page with those guide words.

A. lead—lease
(lean)
(leap)
left
leaf

B. crocus—crossing
cricket
(crop)
(croquet)
(cross)

C. gift—globe
giant
(give)
glove
(glass)

D. rude—rummy
royal
(ruler)
(ruin)
ruby

66

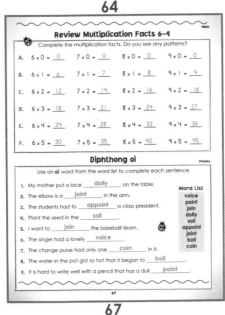

Review Multiplication Facts 6–9
Math

Complete the multiplication facts. Do you see any patterns?

A. 6 × 0 = 0 7 × 0 = 0 8 × 0 = 0 9 × 0 = 0
B. 6 × 1 = 6 7 × 1 = 7 8 × 1 = 8 9 × 1 = 9
C. 6 × 2 = 12 7 × 2 = 14 8 × 2 = 16 9 × 2 = 18
D. 6 × 3 = 18 7 × 3 = 21 8 × 3 = 24 9 × 3 = 27
E. 6 × 4 = 24 7 × 4 = 28 8 × 4 = 32 9 × 4 = 36
F. 6 × 5 = 30 7 × 5 = 35 8 × 5 = 40 9 × 5 = 45

Diphthong oi
Phonics

Use an **oi** word from the word list to complete each sentence.

1. My mother put a lace doily on the table.
2. The elbow is a joint in the arm.
3. The students had to appoint a class president.
4. Plant the seed in the soil.
5. I want to join the baseball team.
6. The singer had a lovely voice.
7. The change purse had only one coin in it.
8. The water in the pot got so hot that it began to boil.
9. It is hard to write well with a pencil that has a dull point.

Word List: voice, point, join, doily, soil, appoint, joint, boil, coin

67

Diphthong ou
Phonics

Write each **ou** word from the word list under its rhyming word. Circle the **ou** diphthong in each word.

Word List: sound, sprout, pout, trout, stout, bound, round, about, surround, shout, pound, hound

scout — sound, sprout
sprout — sound
pout — bound
trout — round
stout — surround
about — pound
shout — hound

mound
sound
bound
round
surround
pound
hound

Review Multiplication Facts 6–9
Math

Circle the correct product for each multiplication fact.

A. 6 × 7 = (42) / 12
B. 9 × 6 = 11 / (54)
C. 4 × 6 = (24) / 16
D. 4 × 7 = 28 / (40)
E. 8 × 8 = 40 / (64)
F. 5 × 9 = 18 / (45)

68

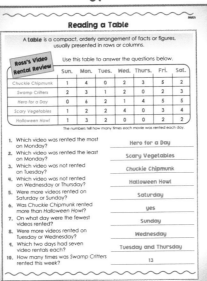

Definitions
Reading Comprehension

Mary Martin, alias Peter Pan

Mary Martin is fondly remembered as the petite star who won an Emmy award for her performance in the TV production of *Peter Pan*. This cheerful, exuberant star was born Mary Virginia Martin on December 1, 1913. When she was 16, she married Benjamin Hagman. They had a son, Larry, who is renowned for his roles in the TV series *I Dream of Jeannie* and *Dallas*. Mary exhibited a talent for aerial ballet. After teaching and performing dance for several years, she journeyed to Hollywood to further her career. She had many roles in films and on Broadway.

Read the paragraph above carefully. Write the letter of the definition on the line next to each numbered word.

1. fondly — d — a. traveled
2. petite — h — b. job, occupation
3. performance — i — c. well known, famous
4. exuberant — e — d. lovingly
5. renowned — c — e. enthusiastic
6. roles — g — f. in the air
7. exhibited — j — g. parts or characters played by an actor
8. aerial — f — h. small, little
9. journeyed — a — i. the act of performing
10. career — b — j. showed or displayed

69

Reading a Table
Math

A **table** is a compact, orderly arrangement of facts or figures, usually presented in rows or columns.

Ross's Video Rental Review

Use this table to answer the questions below.

	Sun.	Mon.	Tues.	Wed.	Thurs.	Fri.	Sat.
Chuckie Chipmunk	1	4	0	2	3	5	2
Swamp Critters	2	3	1	2	0	2	3
Hero for a Day	0	6	2	1	4	5	5
Scary Vegetables	1	2	2	4	0	3	4
Halloween Howl	1	3	2	0	0	2	2

The numbers tell how many times each movie was rented each day.

1. Which video was rented the most on Monday? — Hero for a Day
2. Which video was rented the least on Monday? — Scary Vegetables
3. Which video was not rented on Tuesday? — Chuckie Chipmunk
4. Which video was not rented on Wednesday or Thursday? — Halloween Howl
5. Were more videos rented on Saturday or Sunday? — Saturday
6. Was Chuckie Chipmunk rented more than Halloween Howl? — yes
7. On what day were the fewest videos rented? — Sunday
8. Were more videos rented on Tuesday or Wednesday? — Wednesday
9. Which two days had seven video rentals each? — Tuesday and Thursday
10. How many times was *Swamp Critters* rented this week? — 13

71

Beat the Clock (Multiplication Facts Review)
Math

A. 9 × 1 = 9 5 × 8 = 40 2 × 5 = 10 7 × 5 = 35 4 × 7 = 28
B. 0 × 5 = 0 8 × 0 = 0 6 × 8 = 48 0 × 9 = 0 6 × 3 = 18
C. 9 × 5 = 45 7 × 4 = 28 7 × 0 = 0 4 × 4 = 16 0 × 3 = 0
D. 6 × 4 = 24 1 × 7 = 7 3 × 7 = 21 3 × 1 = 3 5 × 3 = 15
E. 9 × 9 = 81 9 × 3 = 27 0 × 4 = 0 7 × 9 = 63 6 × 0 = 0
F. 1 × 3 = 3 4 × 8 = 32 5 × 7 = 35 5 × 2 = 10 2 × 1 = 2
G. 4 × 9 = 36 1 × 0 = 0 7 × 1 = 7 0 × 0 = 0 3 × 6 = 18
H. 4 × 3 = 12 7 × 8 = 56 2 × 4 = 8 8 × 5 = 40 1 × 2 = 2
I. 3 × 8 = 24 9 × 8 = 72 5 × 1 = 5 3 × 0 = 0 7 × 3 = 21
J. 8 × 1 = 8 5 × 6 = 30 2 × 0 = 0 6 × 2 = 12 0 × 8 = 0
K. 9 × 7 = 63 0 × 1 = 0 6 × 6 = 36 1 × 6 = 6 2 × 0 = 0
L. 9 × 6 = 54 3 × 2 = 6 3 × 5 = 15 4 × 6 = 24
M. 7 × 2 = 14 2 × 6 = 12 0 × 7 = 0 3 × 5 = 15 4 × 6 = 24
N. 2 × 3 = 6 5 × 9 = 45 4 × 2 = 8 1 × 1 = 1 7 × 7 = 49
O. 6 × 5 = 30 0 × 6 = 0 5 × 5 = 25 9 × 2 = 18 8 × 2 = 16
P. 9 × 3 = 27 6 × 1 = 6 5 × 4 = 20 2 × 8 = 16
Q. 1 × 4 = 4 1 × 9 = 9 4 × 9 = 36 0 × 2 = 0 6 × 7 = 42
R. 8 × 4 = 32 4 × 5 = 20 7 × 6 = 42 9 × 5 = 45 5 × 4 = 20
S. 8 × 8 = 64 6 × 8 = 48 9 × 0 = 0 9 × 4 = 36 8 × 7 = 56
T. 3 × 4 = 12 4 × 1 = 4 2 × 7 = 14 8 × 3 = 24 1 × 8 = 8

Time: _____ Number correct: _____

72

Secret Codes and Puzzles

Use the secret code to solve the riddle.

What would your nose be if it were 12 inches long?

FOOT

73

Use the secret code to solve the riddle.

What kind of house is the easiest to lift?

A LIGHT HOUSE

There is enough corn for each crow to have two ears.

There is not enough corn for each crow to have two ears.

74

Use the secret code to solve the riddle.

What's worse than a giraffe with a sore throat?

A CENTIPEDE WITH SORE FEET

75

Color a path across and down to move from start to finish.

Use the secret code to solve the riddle.

What is yellow, weighs 1,000 pounds, and sings?

TWO CANARIES

FIVE-HUNDRED POUND

76

Multiplication Facts 0–9 Review

Problem List

Multiply to solve the problems in the problem list. Then, find the same problems in the puzzle. Circle the hidden problems and write x and = in the correct places. Problems are hidden across and down.

$9 \times 1 = 9$
$8 \times 5 = 40$ $8 \times 8 = 40$
$7 \times 5 = 35$ $9 \times 9 = 81$
$9 \times 3 = 27$ $3 \times 8 = 24$
$7 \times 7 = 49$ $4 \times 9 = 36$
$6 \times 6 = 36$ $3 \times 6 = 18$
$7 \times 4 = 28$ $3 \times 6 = 0$
$8 \times 4 = 32$ $9 \times 4 = 36$
$9 \times 2 = 18$ $9 \times 5 = 45$
$8 \times 8 = 64$ $9 \times 7 = 63$

77

Multiplying One- and Two-Digit Numbers

Rule: Multiply ones, then regroup. Multiply tens, then add extra tens.

Example:
23 × 6 = 138

Solve each problem. Write the answer in the space provided.

A. $10 \times 5 = 50$ B. $10 \times 3 = 30$ C. $12 \times 2 = 24$ D. $15 \times 4 = 60$ E. $19 \times 2 = 38$ F. $31 \times 4 = 124$

G. $62 \times 2 = 124$ H. $27 \times 3 = 81$ I. $54 \times 3 = 162$ J. $79 \times 3 = 237$ L. $87 \times 5 = 435$ M. $90 \times 4 = 360$

Diphthong ow

Write each word from the word list beside its rhyming word. Circle the **ow** diphthong in each word on the line.

Word List: brow, powder, scowl, town, tower

prowl — scowl
power — tower
bow — brow
down — town
powder — powder

BONUS Write another word with an **ow** diphthong to rhyme with each word in the above activity.

79

Drawing Conclusions

Read the story. Then, answer the questions.

Photograph

Jack was not comfortable. His new shirt was too stiff and his tie felt tight. Mother had fussed over his hair trying to get it to look just right. She made him scrub his hands three times to get the dirt from under his fingernails! Finally, his mom said he was ready. She smiled and said that Jack looked very handsome. Jack frowned, but knew he could not tell his mom how he felt. This was important to her. Jack sat on a special stool that turned and looked at the camera. He didn't feel like smiling, but he did his best. "Perfect!" said the man behind the camera as he snapped the shot. Jack posed two more times and then the man said they were finished. The first thing Jack did was take off his tie!

1. What was Jack doing?
He was having his picture taken.

2. What clues tell you where Jack is?
sitting on the stool, looking at the camera

3. How does Jack feel about this?
He does not want to do it.

4. What clues tell you how Jack feels?
His shirt was too stiff. His tie was too tight.

5. Who was the man that said "perfect"?
the photographer

6. Why did Jack take off his tie?
It was not comfortable.

80

Counting Syllables

Syllables represent the number of vowel sounds heard in words.

Examples: what – 1 vowel sound and 1 syllable
pencil – 2 vowel sounds and 2 syllables
animal – 3 vowel sounds and 3 syllables

Read each word below and use the line to write the number of syllables in the word. Listen to make sure that the number of vowel sounds equals the number of syllables for each word.

1. apple — 2
2. prune — 1
3. cherry — 2
4. banana — 3
5. lemon — 2
6. pear — 1
7. watermelon — 4
8. plum — 1
9. strawberry — 3

Alphabetical Order

To alphabetize titles you need to put small words like A, The, or An at the end of a title.

Example: The Cat in the Hat would be Cat in the Hat, The.

Number the titles from 1 to 9 as they should appear alphabetically.

3 — Charlotte's Friend
1 — Amos Goes Camping
4 — The Chocolate Prize
5 — Harvey's Mystery
8 — The Whale Watchers
6 — A Lion and a Bear
9 — Where the River Ends
2 — Cats for Sale
7 — The Needlefish Return

81

Multiplying One- and Three-Digit Numbers

Rule:
1. Multiply ones, then regroup.
2. Multiply tens, then add extra tens.
3. Multiply hundreds.
4. Regroup as needed.

Example: 453 × 4 = 1,812

Solve the problems. Write the answers in the space provided.

A. $100 \times 3 = 300$ B. $120 \times 2 = 240$ C. $278 \times 4 = 1,112$ D. $329 \times 3 = 987$

E. $422 \times 5 = 2,110$ F. $705 \times 4 = 2,820$ G. $827 \times 9 = 7,443$ H. $926 \times 7 = 6,482$

Understanding What I Read

What Eats the Firefly?

There are very few animals that are not eaten by something. No creature, however, eats the firefly, or lightning bug. The adult firefly has almost no predators. Birds, insect-eating mammals, reptiles, and fish do not eat them. Sharks are also bothered by them. They will swish around wildly and then seem to be paralyzed with fear when fireflies are put in their tank.

Read the paragraph. Then, answer the questions.

1. What is the main idea of the paragraph? No creature eats the firefly
2. What is another name for a firefly? lightning bug
3. Describe what the fearless shark will do if a firefly is in its tank. swish around wildly and then seem to be paralyzed with fear
4. What do you think a predator is? Answers will vary

82

Answer Key

Reading a Bar Graph

This bar graph shows the different eye colors of the children in three third grade classes.

What Color Are Your Eyes?

Look at the graph and answer the following questions.

A. How many children have green eyes? 10

B. How many more children have blue eyes than gray eyes? 5

C. How many more children have brown eyes than blue eyes? 5

D. This graph lists eye color for how many third graders? 55

E. Which two eye colors are found on an equal number of students? green and gray

F. Make one statement about this graph based on the data given. Answers will vary.

83

Diphthong oy

Look at the highlighted letters in each pair of words. Circle the word that is spelled correctly, and then use the word in a sentence.

1. (enjoy) enjoi — Sentences will vary.
2. destroi (destroy)
3. loial (loyal)
4. (royal) roial
5. (annoy) annoi
6. toi (toy)

Multiplying Two- and Three-Digit Numbers

Rule:
1. Multiply ones by ones, tens, and hundreds. Regroup as needed.
2. Multiply tens by ones, tens, and hundreds. Regroup as needed.
3. Add the two numbers to find the final product.

Example:
325 × 43; 325 × 43; 325 × 43 = 13,975

Solve the problems.

A. 203 × 12 = 2,436
B. 330 × 25 = 8,250
C. 633 × 61 = 38,613
D. 567 × 38 = 21,546

84

Multiplication Rounding and Estimating

Rule: Since it is easier to multiply by numbers ending in 0, it can be useful to estimate an approximate answer by rounding.

Example: 26 × 9 = ___
26 rounds up to 30, so the estimated product is: 30 × 9 = 270

Round the two-digit factor to the nearest ten. Multiply to find the estimated product.

A. 18→20 × 2→2 = 40
B. 23→20 × 5→5 = 100
C. 15→20 × 3→3 = 60
D. 24→20 × 9→9 = 180
E. 58→60 × 5→5 = 300
F. 64→60 × 7→7 = 420
G. 75→80 × 4→4 = 320
H. 81→80 × 8→8 = 640

Adjectives

Use the line in front of each noun to write an adjective that describes the noun.

1. Answers will vary. rain
2. ___ table
3. ___ flower
4. ___ day
5. ___ fruit
6. ___ petal
7. ___ grass
8. ___ friend
9. ___ lake
10. ___ house

85

Prefixes and Suffixes

Base Words are the root words that are used to make other words.
helpful
The root word is help.

Prefixes are letters that are put in front of base words to change the meaning of the base words.
rewrite
The prefix re changes the meaning of the base word write.

Suffixes are letters added to the end of base words to change the meaning of the base word.
healthy
The suffix y changes the meaning of the base word health.

For each question below, decide which part of the word is highlighted in blue. Write base word, prefix, or suffix on the line.

1. punish**ment** — base word
2. **dark**ness — suffix
3. **dis**appear — prefix
4. **pre**cook — prefix
5. pre**soak** — base word
6. proud**ly** — suffix
7. place**ment** — suffix
8. **dis**trust — prefix
9. color**less** — suffix
10. **friend**ly — base word
11. sick**ness** — base word
12. sugar**less** — base word
13. fool**ish** — suffix
14. **brown**ish — suffix
15. **re**fill — prefix
16. **re**pay — base word
17. **un**sure — prefix
18. **lone**ly — suffix

86

Capitalization

In the story below, circle each letter that should be a capital letter. Add an ending to the story.

my birthday

today is my birthday. i am nine years old. i was born on wednesday, april 12, in billings, montana. my family will celebrate my birthday tonight. mom will cook her special spaghetti dinner just for me. dad will be home from work early. my brother, david, and my sister, rose, will be here, too. after dinner grandma and grandpa will come. we will all eat cake and ice cream. they will sing "happy birthday" to me. then i . . .

Endings will vary.

87

Fact and Opinion

A **fact** is something that is real and could happen.
An **opinion** is something that is believed to be true but may not be.

There are apples on the tree.
Those apples are beautiful.

Mark each sentence with an F for fact or an O for opinion.

F 1. My mother fixes dinner every night at 6:00.
O 2. Chocolate pie is the best dessert.
F 3. The state of Wisconsin is a part of the United States.
F 4. People can go to a movie theater to watch movies.
O 5. It is more fun to rent a movie and watch it at home than to go to a theater.

Problem Solving with Multiplication

Solve the word problems. Show your work and write the answers in the space provided.

A. Sophia's Bakery sold 8 cakes each day for 21 days. How many cakes did the bakery sell in all? 168 cakes

B. Regina made 49 gift baskets each week for 5 weeks. Estimate how many gift baskets she made. 250 gift baskets

C. For 21 days of camp, Melanie collected 2 souvenirs each day. How many souvenirs did she collect in all? 42 souvenirs

D. Donna sold 136 bags of popcorn at the movie theater for 24 days. Estimate to find out about how many bags of popcorn Donna sold. 140 × 20 = 2,800 bags of popcorn

88

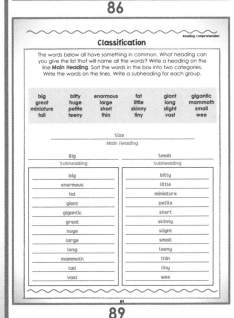

Classification

The words below all have something in common. What heading can you give the list that will name all the words? Write a heading on the line **Main Heading**. Sort the words in the box into two categories. Write the words on the lines. Write a subheading for each group.

big	bitty	enormous	fat	giant	gigantic
great	huge	large	little	long	mammoth
miniature	petite	short	skinny	slight	small
tall	teeny	thin	tiny	vast	wee

Size
Main Heading

Big	Small
Subheading	Subheading
big	bitty
enormous	little
fat	miniature
giant	petite
gigantic	short
great	skinny
huge	slight
large	small
long	teeny
mammoth	thin
tall	tiny
vast	wee

89

Telling Time

Read each problem and circle the correct answer for each.

A. Which clock shows 8:30?
B. Which clock has the same time as the first one?
C. Which clock shows 15 minutes before 7?
D. Quarter past four is another way of saying which of the following times?

Beginning Digraphs: ch, sh, th

Say the name of each picture. Circle the beginning digraph.

1. th
2. sh
3. sh
4. ch

Say the name of each picture. Write the beginning digraph ch, sh, or th to complete the word.

5. ch_urch
6. ch_icken
7. sh_ell
8. th_imble

90

Beginning Digraph ph

Read the words. Underline the beginning digraph **ph** in each word.

1. physical
2. pharmacy
3. photograph
4. pharaoh
5. phantom
6. phonograph
7. physician
8. photosynthesis
9. phonics

Read the words. Circle each word that begins with the digraph **ph**. Place an **x** on any word that does not begin with this digraph.

10. (phony)
11. (photography)
12. piñch
13. poültry
14. pâge
15. (phobia)
16. püddle
17. (pharmacist)
18. (phase)
19. plëase
20. pi$ho
21. pâper

Elapsed Time

Find each time. All times are A.M. Write the answer on the line provided.

A. 30 minutes after — 10:30 A.M.
B. 15 minutes after — 11:45 A.M.
C. 15 minutes after — 5:00 A.M.
D. 30 minutes after — 3:15 A.M.
E. 30 minutes before — 8:15 A.M.
F. 1 hour before — 9:00 A.M.

91

Answer Key

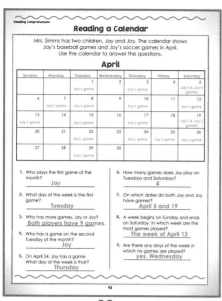

Reading a Calendar

Mrs. Simms has two children, Jay and Joy. The calendar shows Jay's baseball games and Joy's soccer games in April. Use the calendar to answer the questions.

April

Sunday	Monday	Tuesday	Wednesday	Thursday	Friday	Saturday
		1 Joy's game	2	3 Joy's game	4	5 Jay's & Joy's games
6 Joy's game	7 Joy's game	8	9	10 Joy's game	11	12
13 Jay's game	14	15	16	17 Joy's game	18	19 Jay's & Joy's games
20	21	22 Jay's game	23	24 Joy's game	25	26 Jay's game
27	28	29 Joy's game	30			

1. Who plays the first game of the month? **Jay**
2. What day of the week is the first game? **Tuesday**
3. Who has more games, Jay or Joy? **Both players have 9 games.**
4. Who has a game on the second Tuesday of the month? **Joy**
5. On April 24, Joy has a game. What day of the week is that? **Thursday**
6. How many games does Joy play on Tuesdays and Saturdays? **4**
7. On which dates do both Jay and Joy have games? **April 5 and 19**
8. A week begins on Sunday and ends on Saturday. In which week are the most games played? **The week of April 13**
9. Are there any days of the week in which no games are played? **yes, Wednesday**

92

Division Facts 0–1

Rules: 0 divide by any number will always equal 0.
Any number divided by 1 will always equal that number.

Examples: $0 \div 5 = 0$ $8 \div 1 = 8$

A. $0 \div 12 = $ **0** B. $0 \div 10 = $ **0** C. $3 \div 1 = $ **3**
D. $5 \div 1 = $ **5** E. $0 \div 3 = $ **0** F. $0 \div 6 = $ **0**
G. $4 \div 1 = $ **4** H. $0 \div 9 = $ **0** I. $0 \div 1 = $ **0**
J. $11 \div 1 = $ **11** K. $7 \div 1 = $ **7** L. $0 \div 2 = $ **0**
M. $9 \div 1 = $ **9** N. $1 \div 1 = $ **1** O. $0 \div 8 = $ **0**

Beginning Digraph qu

Say the name of each picture. Circle the picture if the word begins with the digraph **qu**. Put an **X** on the picture if the word does not begin with **qu**.

Read each word. If the word begins with the digraph **qu**, write **qu** on the line. If not, leave the line blank.

5. quarrel **qu** 6. quest **qu** 7. shadow
8. suntan 9. quiet **qu** 10. frown
11. quack **qu** 12. powder 13. quality **qu**

94

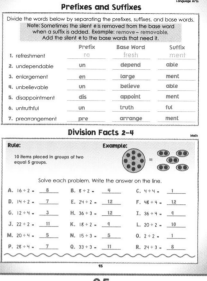

Prefixes and Suffixes

Divide the words below by separating the prefixes, suffixes, and base words.
Note: Sometimes the silent **e** is removed from the base word when a suffix is added. Example: remove – removable. Add the silent **e** to the base words that need it.

	Prefix	Base Word	Suffix
1. refreshment	re	fresh	ment
2. undependable	un	depend	able
3. enlargement	en	large	ment
4. unbelievable	un	believe	able
5. disappointment	dis	appoint	ment
6. untruthful	un	truth	ful
7. prearrangement	pre	arrange	ment

Division Facts 2–4

Rule: 10 items placed in groups of two equal 5 groups. **Example:**

Solve each problem. Write the answer on the line.

A. $16 \div 2 = $ **8** B. $8 \div 2 = $ **4** C. $4 \div 4 = $ **1**
D. $14 \div 2 = $ **7** E. $24 \div 2 = $ **12** F. $48 \div 4 = $ **12**
G. $12 \div 4 = $ **3** H. $36 \div 3 = $ **12** I. $36 \div 4 = $ **9**
J. $22 \div 2 = $ **11** K. $18 \div 2 = $ **9** L. $20 \div 2 = $ **10**
M. $20 \div 4 = $ **5** N. $15 \div 3 = $ **5** O. $2 \div 2 = $ **1**
P. $28 \div 4 = $ **7** Q. $33 \div 3 = $ **11** R. $24 \div 3 = $ **8**

95

Division Facts 1–5

Divide to solve the problems in the problem list. Then, find the same problems in the puzzle. Circle each hidden problem and write ÷ and = in the correct places. Problems are hidden across and down.

Problem List
$6 \div 2 = $ **3**
$4 \div 2 = $ **2**
$3 \div 1 = $ **3**
$15 \div 5 = $ **3**
$20 \div 5 = $ **4**
$25 \div 5 = $ **5**
$10 \div 2 = $ **5**
$8 \div 4 = $ **2**
$9 \div 3 = $ **3**
$20 \div 4 = $ **5**
$15 \div 5 = $ **3**
$12 \div 3 = $ **4**
$12 \div 6 = $ **2**
$5 \div 5 = $ **1**
$10 \div 5 = $ **2**
$8 \div 2 = $ **4**
$6 \div 3 = $ **2**
$16 \div 4 = $ **4**

96

Division Facts 5–7

Solve each problem. Then, write the answer on the line provided.

A. $30 \div 5 = $ **6** $54 \div 6 = $ **9** $49 \div 7 = $ **7**
B. $12 \div 6 = $ **2** $15 \div 5 = $ **3** $60 \div 6 = $ **10**
C. $40 \div 5 = $ **8** $28 \div 7 = $ **4** $25 \div 5 = $ **5**
D. $18 \div 6 = $ **2** $70 \div 7 = $ **10** $60 \div 5 = $ **12**
E. $42 \div 6 = $ **7** $63 \div 7 = $ **9** $77 \div 7 = $ **11**
F. $35 \div 7 = $ **5** $7 \div 7 = $ **1** $14 \div 7 = $ **2**
G. $48 \div 6 = $ **8** $36 \div 6 = $ **6** $10 \div 5 = $ **2**
H. $20 \div 5 = $ **4** $55 \div 5 = $ **11** $84 \div 7 = $ **12**
I. $56 \div 7 = $ **8** $45 \div 5 = $ **9** $66 \div 6 = $ **11**

97

Ending Blend -mp

Add the ending blend **mp** to each set of letters. Say the words.

1. bu **mp** 2. ca **mp** 3. stu **mp** 4. lu **mp**
5. swa **mp** 6. shri **mp** 7. pu **mp** 8. cla **mp**

Look at each picture. Circle the **mp** word that names each picture and write the word on the line.

9. limp (blimp) skimp — **blimp** 10. (jump) pump lump — **jump** 11. camp (lamp) ramp — **lamp**

Sequencing

Read the poem below to find out what was wrong with Buzzy's car. Read the sentences next to the poem. Decide what happened first, second, and so on. Number the sentences in the correct order.

Buzzy's New Car

7 Buzzy's hair turned gray.
4 The engine broke down.
2 Buzzy bought a car.
6 A second tire went "POP!"
1 Buzzy saved his money.
3 The radiator cracked.
5 Buzzy pushed the car off the road.

98

Division Facts 8–9

Solve each problem. Write the answer on the line provided.

A. $16 \div 8 = $ **2** $24 \div 8 = $ **3** $54 \div 9 = $ **6**
B. $36 \div 9 = $ **4** $72 \div 9 = $ **8** $56 \div 8 = $ **7**
C. $88 \div 8 = $ **11** $32 \div 8 = $ **4** $72 \div 8 = $ **9**
D. $45 \div 9 = $ **5** $81 \div 9 = $ **9** $80 \div 8 = $ **10**
E. $27 \div 9 = $ **3** $90 \div 9 = $ **10** $96 \div 8 = $ **12**
F. $40 \div 8 = $ **5** $64 \div 8 = $ **8** $63 \div 9 = $ **7**
G. $8 \div 8 = $ **1** $18 \div 9 = $ **2** $108 \div 9 = $ **12**
H. $48 \div 8 = $ **6** $9 \div 9 = $ **1** $99 \div 9 = $ **11**

99

Division Facts 1–9

Divide to solve the problems and then color.

4 = red 7 = orange
5 = purple 6 = red rose
black

100

Beat the Clock (Division Facts 1–4)

A.
$5\overline{)10}$ **2** $4\overline{)28}$ **7** $2\overline{)4}$ **2** $9\overline{)36}$ **4** $6\overline{)30}$ **5** $4\overline{)16}$ **4** $9\overline{)0}$ **0** $3\overline{)15}$ **5** $8\overline{)72}$ **9** $6\overline{)18}$ **3**

B.
$8\overline{)48}$ **6** $3\overline{)6}$ **2** $7\overline{)21}$ **3** $1\overline{)3}$ **3** $7\overline{)56}$ **8** $6\overline{)0}$ **0** $2\overline{)16}$ **8** $6\overline{)54}$ **9** $1\overline{)7}$ **7** $9\overline{)45}$ **5**

C.
$7\overline{)49}$ **7** $5\overline{)35}$ **7** $3\overline{)24}$ **8** $7\overline{)7}$ **1** $3\overline{)12}$ **4** $8\overline{)24}$ **3** $1\overline{)1}$ **1** $9\overline{)72}$ **8** $7\overline{)35}$ **5** $5\overline{)25}$ **5**

D.
$9\overline{)27}$ **3** $1\overline{)0}$ **0** $8\overline{)40}$ **5** $5\overline{)15}$ **3** $2\overline{)2}$ **1** $6\overline{)48}$ **8** $5\overline{)0}$ **0** $4\overline{)24}$ **6** $2\overline{)8}$ **4** $5\overline{)15}$ **3**

E.
$7\overline{)49}$ **7** $6\overline{)12}$ **2** $3\overline{)3}$ **1** $2\overline{)12}$ **6** $9\overline{)9}$ **1** $5\overline{)4}$ **4** $6\overline{)24}$ **4** $4\overline{)4}$ **1** $8\overline{)64}$ **8** $5\overline{)45}$ **9**

F.
$2\overline{)6}$ **3** $6\overline{)24}$ **4** $4\overline{)12}$ **3** $3\overline{)0}$ **0** $8\overline{)4}$ **4** $4\overline{)36}$ **9** $2\overline{)0}$ **0** $7\overline{)28}$ **4** $9\overline{)63}$ **7** $3\overline{)21}$ **7**

G.
$6\overline{)42}$ **7** $5\overline{)25}$ **5** $1\overline{)8}$ **8** $9\overline{)54}$ **6** $3\overline{)27}$ **9** $5\overline{)0}$ **0** $1\overline{)5}$ **5** $5\overline{)40}$ **8** $1\overline{)4}$ **4** $7\overline{)0}$ **0**

H.
$4\overline{)32}$ **8** $2\overline{)18}$ **9** $9\overline{)81}$ **9** $8\overline{)56}$ **7** $9\overline{)9}$ **1** $1\overline{)3}$ **3** $2\overline{)14}$ **7** $9\overline{)36}$ **4** $4\overline{)8}$ **2** $8\overline{)16}$ **2**

I.
$7\overline{)14}$ **2** $8\overline{)48}$ **6** $5\overline{)20}$ **4** $4\overline{)16}$ **4** $9\overline{)9}$ **1** $8\overline{)0}$ **0** $5\overline{)30}$ **6** $7\overline{)0}$ **0** $9\overline{)9}$ **1** $8\overline{)32}$ **4**

J.
$1\overline{)6}$ **6** $6\overline{)54}$ **9** $6\overline{)36}$ **6** $3\overline{)18}$ **6** $7\overline{)63}$ **9** $4\overline{)8}$ **2** $2\overline{)10}$ **5** $7\overline{)42}$ **6** $9\overline{)18}$ **2** $4\overline{)20}$ **5**

Time: _____ Number correct: _____

103

154

Answer Key

Ending Blend -nd

Look at the pictures and say the words.
Circle the **nd** word that names each picture.

Read each sentence. Circle the **nd** word that completes the sentence.
4. We left at the _____ of the movie.
5. Be careful when you _____ on the stool.
6. I saw a penny on the _____.
7. Guide dogs help the _____.

Decimal Place Value

Rule:	Example:
The decimal point separates the ones digit from the tenths digit.	23.45 = 2 3 . 4 5

Underline the digit in the tenths place.
A. 38.15 B. 11.18 C. 65.56 D. 50.63
E. 10.93 F. 9.95 G. 19.81 H. 19.58

Underline the digit in the hundredths place.
I. 19.62 J. 6.78 K. 73.17 L. 35.18
M. 25.84 N. 22.15 O. 99.99 P. 18.33

104

Proofreading

Add punctuation marks and capital letters where they are needed in the story below. Add an ending to the story.

Stories will vary.

105

Vocabulary Assessment

Read the first part of each sentence. Choose the word that means about the same thing as the highlighted word or phrase. Fill in the circle next to the correct answer.

1. To wash or clean by rubbing hard is to . . . — scrub
2. A group of related sentences is a . . . — paragraph
3. When you get something, you . . . — receive
4. The smallest amount is the . . . — least
5. Two things that are completely different are called . . . — opposite
6. To be thankful is to be . . . — grateful
7. Anything that happened before now is the . . . — past
8. A book that lists meanings of words is a . . . — dictionary
9. When you stay behind, you . . . — remain
10. To make a person do something he doesn't want to do is to . . . — force

107

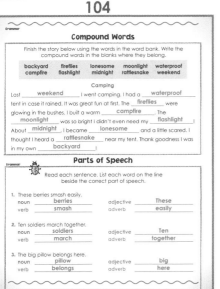

Compound Words

Finish the story below using the words in the word bank. Write the compound words in the blanks where they belong.

backyard fireflies lonesome moonlight waterproof
campfire flashlight midnight rattlesnake weekend

Camping

Last **weekend** I went camping. I had a **waterproof** tent in case it rained. It was great fun at first. The **fireflies** were glowing in the bushes. I built a warm **campfire**. The **moonlight** was so bright I didn't even need my **flashlight**. About **midnight**, I became **lonesome** and a little scared. I thought I heard a **rattlesnake** near my tent. Thank goodness I was in my own **backyard**.

Parts of Speech

Read each sentence. List each word on the line beside the correct part of speech.

1. These berries smash easily.
noun berries adjective These
verb smash adverb easily
2. Ten soldiers march together.
noun soldiers adjective Ten
verb march adverb together
3. The big pillow belongs here.
noun pillow adjective big
verb belongs adverb here

108

Reading and Writing Decimals

Decimals are numbers used to represent fractions. They contain a decimal point. Change the numbers below from word form to decimals.

Example: six and five-tenths is written 6.5

A. two-tenths .2
B. five-tenths .5
C. seven-hundredths .07
D. one and nine-hundredths 1.09
E. four and six-tenths 4.6
F. fifteen and eight-hundredths 15.08

Ending Blends: -lk, -nk, -sk

Say the name of each picture. Circle the word that names the picture and underline the ending.

Circle the ending blend in each word.
4. ki sk 5. to lk 6. hu sk 7. thi nk
8. fri sk 9. wi nk 10. su lk 11. bli nk
12. ta lk 13. ya nk 14. bri sk 15. sku lk

109

Cause and Effect

A **cause** is the reason something happens.
An **effect** is what happens.

Example:
The cat scratched me because I pulled its tail.
Cause—I pulled its tail.
Effect—The cat scratched me.

Underline the **cause** in each sentence.
1. The rain started, and the boys ran for shelter.
2. Mother served ice cream and cake after dinner because it is my favorite dessert.
3. Since I cannot swim, my dad will not let me go to the lake by myself.
4. Joshua sleeps most of the day because he is a baby.
5. Mary cannot go to school because she is sick.

Circle the **effect** in each sentence.
6. Noel went to the movies this afternoon because she was bored.
7. I was so tired that I went to bed early last night.
8. Since she had work to do, Anna did not watch television today.
9. I made an A on my test because I studied.
10. I skinned my knee when I fell off my bike.

110

Crossword Puzzles

111

112

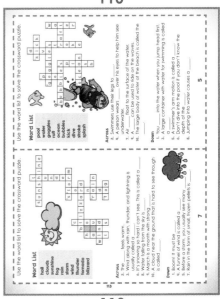

113

155

Answer Key

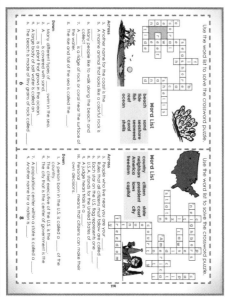

114

Ending Blends: -ft, -nt, -st

Say the name of each picture.
Write the ending blends, **ft**, **nt**, or **st**, to complete the word.

1. li **st** 2. fore **st** 3. te **nt** 4. pla **nt**
5. a **nt** 6. wri **st** 7. gi **ft** 8. ne **st**

Adding and Subtracting Decimals

Rule:
1. Line up the decimal points.
2. Start from the far right.
3. Regroup as needed.
4. Bring the decimal point down to the answer.

Example: 3.76 + 1.59 =

$$3.76 + 1.59 = 5.35$$

A.	B.	C.	D.
6.5 +7.3 = 13.8	2.7 +4.1 = 6.8	6.5 -1.2 = 5.3	5.9 -2.5 = 3.4

E.	F.	G.	H.
12.5 +9.4 = 21.9	0.42 +0.36 = .78	2.41 +7.49 = 9.90	5.7 +8.5 = 14.2

I.	J.	K.	L.
3.8 +4.9 = 8.7	10.5 -7.7 = 2.8	4.13 -2.95 = 1.18	0.28 +.87 = 1.15

116

Persuasive Paragraphs

You must convince your mom to let you play in the rain.
Give your reasons. Then, ask again.

Title	
Question	May I
Reasons	1.
	2.
	Details will vary.
	3.
	4.
Ask again	

Use the sentences above to write a paragraph. Ask the question, state the reasons, and then ask the question again. Indent the first sentence. Use capital letters and periods. Remember to give your paragraph a title.

Paragraphs will vary.

117

Syllables

Find out how many syllables are in each word by counting the number of vowels you hear when you say the word. Write the number on the blank.

1. machine — 2 2. somersault — 3 3. peanut — 2
4. neighborhood — 3 5. astronaut — 3 6. koala — 3
7. dragon — 2 8. itch — 1 9. hero — 2
10. auditorium — 5 11. longitude — 3 12. congratulate — 4
13. frog — 1 14. multiplication — 5 15. Canada — 3
16. zipper — 2 17. gulf — 1 18. lasagna — 3

Adding and Subtracting Fractions

Rule:
When adding or subtracting fractions with the same denominator:
1. Add or subtract their numerators.
2. Write that number over the same denominator.

Examples:
$$\frac{3}{8} + \frac{2}{8} = \frac{5}{8}$$
$$\frac{9}{10} - \frac{3}{10} = \frac{6}{10}$$

Solve each problem. Write the answer in the space provided.

A. $\frac{4}{7} - \frac{2}{7} = \frac{2}{7}$ B. $\frac{1}{3} + \frac{1}{3} = \frac{2}{3}$ C. $\frac{7}{8} - \frac{5}{8} = \frac{2}{8}$

D. $\frac{3}{11} + \frac{5}{11} = \frac{8}{11}$ E. $\frac{10}{25} - \frac{3}{25} = \frac{7}{25}$ F. $\frac{1}{5} - \frac{1}{5} = 0$

118

Writing Stories

Write a story about the picture. Be sure to use capital letters and periods where needed. Give your story a title.

Things to Think About
Who is this story about?
Where does this story take place?
How does the story begin?
What happens next?
How will the story end?

Stories will vary.

119

Division

Example:
$$6\overline{)30} = 5, \ -30, \ 0$$

Think: 6 divides evenly into 30, leaving no remainder.

Solve the problems.

A. $5\overline{)35} = 7$ B. $7\overline{)14} = 2$ C. $4\overline{)28} = 7$ D. $3\overline{)24} = 8$

E. $3\overline{)18} = 6$ F. $8\overline{)56} = 7$ G. $3\overline{)33} = 11$ H. $8\overline{)64} = 8$

Synonyms

Synonyms are words that have the same or almost the same meaning.

Examples: work – toil, small – little

Circle the two words in each row that are synonyms.

1. **beautiful** — clever — **pretty** — eager
2. **wicked** — **evil** — curious — calm
3. hymn — **honor** — fall — **respect**
4. sing — volley — **clap** — **applaud**
5. **get** — return — area — **receive**
6. **unhappy** — tender — shock — **sad**
7. end — **plead** — **beg** — cause

120

Ending Digraphs: -ch, -sh, -th

Say the name of each picture.
Circle the word that names the picture and write the word.

1. much / which / **couch** — couch
2. **brush** / wish / dish — brush
3. broth / with / **mouth** — mouth
4. wreath / **bath** / sloth — bath
5. teach / **peach** / beach — peach
6. rush / **bush** / ash — bush

Division with No Remainders

Example:
$$4\overline{)48} = 12, \ -4, \ 08, \ -8, \ 0$$

Think: 4 divides evenly into 48, leaving no remainder.

Solve the problems.

A. $2\overline{)64} = 32$ B. $9\overline{)90} = 10$ C. $6\overline{)72} = 12$ D. $4\overline{)100} = 25$

E. $3\overline{)69} = 23$ F. $3\overline{)36} = 12$ G. $6\overline{)84} = 14$ H. $5\overline{)125} = 25$

121

Division with Remainders

Example:
$$4\overline{)35} = 8 \ R3, \ -32, \ 3$$

Think: 35 divided by 4 is 8 because 8 × 4 is closest to 35 without exceeding 35.
Then, 35 – 32 is 3, and 3 is called the **remainder**.

Solve the problems

A. $4\overline{)75} = 18R3$ B. $6\overline{)63} = 10R3$ C. $9\overline{)98} = 10R8$ D. $7\overline{)87} = 12R3$

E. $3\overline{)52} = 17R1$ F. $8\overline{)89} = 11R1$ G. $3\overline{)34} = 11R1$ H. $2\overline{)39} = 19R1$

Ending Digraph -ng

Read the **ng** words. Circle the ending digraph and draw a line from each word to its description.

1. ba **ng** — D. a loud noise
2. fa **ng** — C. a sharp, pointy tooth
3. ri **ng** — A. a piece of jewelry worn on the finger
4. wi **ng** — B. the part of a bird that helps it fly

Look at the pictures and say the **ng** words.
Circle the **ng** word that names each picture.

5. hang / gong / **sing**
6. wrong / **king** / long
7. **swing** / lung / strong

122

Ending Digraph -dge

Read the words. Circle each word that ends with the digraph **dge**.

1. **sludge** 2. clay 3. **partridge** 4. insect
5. **ridge** 6. wade 7. **fudge** 8. age
9. **lodge** 10. **hedge** 11. sled 12. ride

Look at the pictures and say the words. Fill in the circle next to the **dge** word that names each picture.

13. ● badge / ○ edge
14. ● judge / ○ fudge
15. ○ lodge / ● bridge

Problem Solving with Division

Solve the problems. Show your work.

A. Stan had 32 bags of popcorn to sell at the snack bar. He sold all of the popcorn to 8 customers. If each customer bought the same number of popcorn bags, how many bags did each buy?
4 popcorn bags

B. Ms. Davis drove 325 miles in 5 days. If she drove the same number of miles each day, how many miles did she drive?
65 miles

C. Phil sold 146 magazine subscriptions. He worked for 2 weeks and sold the same amount each week. How many subscriptions did he sell each week?
73 subscriptions

D. Reginald has 162 seeds to plant in his garden. If he digs 18 holes in the soil and wants to distribute the seeds equally, how many seeds can he put in each hole?
9 seeds

123

Answer Key

Problem Solving with Decimals

A. Complete the next 3 decimals in each sequence.

.15, .25, .35, .45, __55__ __65__ __75__

3.8, 3.7, 3.6, 3.5, __3.4__ __3.3__ __3.2__

B. Using the greater than (>) and less than (<) symbols, write two number sentences using the following numbers: 3.4, 3.5

3.4 < 3.5
3.5 < 3.4

C. Place the following numbers in order from least to greatest.

2.5, 5.2, 4.2, 4.12, 5.25

__2.5__ , __4.12__ , __4.2__ , __5.2__ , __5.25__

D. Chuck's weekly allowance is $5.00. After buying a package of beef jerky for $1.67, how much money does he have left?

$5.00
−1.67
$3.33

Antonyms

Antonyms are words that have opposite meanings.
Examples: hot – cold, near – far

Circle the two words in each row that are antonyms.

1. juggle ⟨approve⟩ explode ⟨dislike⟩
2. grasp fact ⟨achieve⟩ ⟨fail⟩
3. sure blot ⟨calm⟩ ⟨stormy⟩
4. ⟨even⟩ escape plain ⟨uneven⟩
5. ⟨wrong⟩ call wait ⟨right⟩
6. ⟨shame⟩ ⟨honor⟩ helpful below

124

Sequencing

Sequencing means to put things in the proper order.

The hot chocolate recipe in the box is all mixed up. After reading all the steps, put the recipe in the correct order. Some steps have already been written.

Hot Chocolate for Cold Days

Pour a cup of water into a pan and heat it until it is boiling.
Put 3 tablespoons of hot chocolate mix into the mug.
Pour the heated water into the mug and stir.
Place a marshmallow on top and drink.
Turn off the stove and remove the hot water.
Take out a mug, a spoon, and hot chocolate mix and set aside.

1. Take out a mug, a spoon, and hot chocolate mix and set aside.
2. Pour a cup of water into a pan and heat it until it is boiling.
3. Put 3 tablespoons of hot chocolate mix into the mug.
4. Turn off the stove and remove the hot water.
5. Pour the heated water into the mug and stir.
6. Place a marshmallow on top and drink.

125

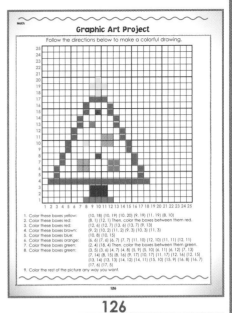

Graphic Art Project

Follow the directions below to make a colorful drawing.

1. Color these boxes yellow: (10, 18), (10, 19) (9, 19), (1, 19), (8, 10)
2. Color these boxes red: (8, 1), (12, 1) Then, color the boxes between them red.
3. Color these boxes red: (12, 6) (12, 7) (13, 6) (13, 7), (9, 13)
4. Color these boxes brown: (9, 2), (10, 2), (11, 2), (9, 3), (10, 3), (11, 3)
5. Color these boxes blue: (10, 8) (10, 15)
6. Color these boxes orange: (6, 6), (6, 7), (7, 7) (11, 10), (12, 10), (11, 11), (12, 11)
7. Color these boxes green: (2, 4), (18, 4) Then, color the boxes between them green.
8. Color these boxes green: (3, 5) (3, 6) (4, 7) (4, 8) (5, 9) (5, 10) (6, 11) (6, 12) (7, 13) (7, 14) (8, 15) (8, 16) (9, 17) (11, 17) (12, 16) (13, 15) (14, 13) (13, 14) (14, 12) (14, 11) (15, 10) (15, 9) (16, 8) (16, 7) (17, 6) (17, 5)
9. Color the rest of the picture any way you want.

126

Silent Letter in "tch"

Read the words. If the word ends with the digraph **tch**, fill in the circle and circle the ending digraph.

1. pi⟨tch⟩ ● 2. search ○ 3. hu⟨tch⟩ ● 4. fight ○
5. with ○ 6. such ○ 7. wrath ○ 8. twi⟨tch⟩ ●
9. pa⟨tch⟩ ● 10. ha⟨tch⟩ ● 11. fe⟨tch⟩ ● 12. clutch ○

Say the name of each picture. Circle the word that names the picture.

13. hatch ⟨watch⟩ catch
14. ⟨stretch⟩ itch blotch
15. batch ⟨crutch⟩ stitch

Perimeter

Perimeter is the measurement of the length around a figure. You can find the perimeter by adding the lengths of all the sides.

Look at the following figures and find the perimeter of each.

A. (square, sides 2, 2, 2, 2)
Perimeter = __8__ units

B. (rectangle, 4, 2, 4, 2)
Perimeter = __12__ units

131

Subject-Verb Agreement

Complete each sentence with the correct verb form.

1. In the summer, I __work__ as a detective. [work / works]
2. I __solve__ neighborhood mysteries. [solve / solves]
3. When Mrs. Carter __loses__ her cat, I help her find it. [lose / loses]
4. If there are footprints, I __find__ out whose they are. [find / finds]
5. My friend Jim __writes__ me secret messages. [write / writes]
6. I __use__ my decoder to figure them out. [use / uses]
7. I __keep__ my detective kit in a secret place. [keep / keeps]
8. Only Mom and Dad __know__ where it is. [know / knows]

Predicting

Read the paragraph. Then answer the questions.

The children were playing baseball in the empty lot. Peggy was at bat. She swung hard and hit the ball farther than anyone else had. The ball sailed across the lot and smashed through Mrs. Allen's window. Peggy knew Mrs. Allen would be really angry. The other kids scattered, running for home. Peggy looked at the broken window.

1. What do you think Peggy will do?
Answers will vary.

2. Which clues helped you to decide?
Answers will vary.

132

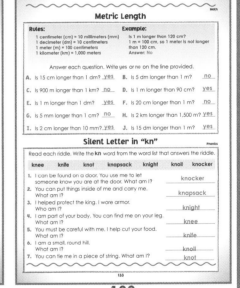

Metric Length

Rules:
1 centimeter (cm) = 10 millimeters (mm)
1 decimeter (dm) = 10 centimeters
1 meter (m) = 100 centimeters
1 kilometer (km) = 1,000 meters

Example:
Is 1 m longer than 120 cm?
1 m = 100 cm, so 1 meter is not longer than 120 cm.
Answer: No

Answer each question. Write yes or no on the line provided.

A. Is 15 cm longer than 1 dm? __yes__
B. Is 5 dm longer than 1 m? __no__
C. Is 900 m longer than 1 km? __no__
D. Is 1 m longer than 90 cm? __yes__
E. Is 1 m longer than 1 dm? __yes__
F. Is 20 cm longer than 1 m? __no__
G. Is 5 mm longer than 1 cm? __no__
H. Is 2 km longer than 1,500 m? __yes__
I. Is 2 cm longer than 10 mm? __yes__
J. Is 15 cm longer than 1 m? __yes__

Silent Letter in "kn"

Read each riddle. Write the **kn** word from the word list that answers the riddle.

| knee | knife | knot | knapsack | knight | knoll | knocker |

1. I can be found on a door. You use me to let someone know you are at the door. What am I? __knocker__
2. You can put things inside of me and carry me. What am I? __knapsack__
3. I helped protect the king. I wore armor. Who am I? __knight__
4. I am part of your body. You can find me on your leg. What am I? __knee__
5. You must be careful with me. I help cut your food. What am I? __knife__
6. I am a small, round hill. What am I? __knoll__
7. You can tie me in a piece of string. What am I? __knot__

133

Silent Letter in "wr"

Write the letters **wr** in front of each set of letters. Say the words.

1. __wr__ inkle 2. __wr__ eath 3. __wr__ ong 4. __wr__ angle
5. __wr__ apper 6. __wr__ eck 7. __wr__ estle 8. __wr__ ap

Say each **wr** word. Circle the picture of the word.

9. wrap 10. wrist 11. write 12. wring

Customary Length

Using an inch ruler, measure each line segment to the nearest inch. Write the answer in the box to the right of the segment.

A. 1
B. 2
C. 3
D. 4
E. 5
F. 6

134

Customary Capacity

Rules:
2 cups = 1 pint
2 pints = 1 quart
4 quarts = 1 gallon

Example:
Is one cup greater than, less than, or equal to 1 pint?
If 2 cups = 1 pint
then 1 cup is __less than__ 1 pint.

Complete each sentence using **more than**, **less than**, or **equal to**. Write your answer on the line.

A. 2 pints are __equal to__ 1 quart.
B. 1 pint is __less than__ 1 quart.
C. 3 quarts are __less than__ 1 gallon.
D. 3 cups are __less than__ 1 quart.
E. 1 gallon is __more than__ 1 pint.
F. 6 pints are __equal to__ 3 quarts.
G. 2 pints are __equal to__ 4 cups.
H. 8 quarts are __equal to__ 2 gallons.

Silent Letter in "ck"

Read the words. Circle each word that ends with the letters **ck**.

1. jazz 2. speech 3. mask 4. crutch
5. ⟨rock⟩ 6. ⟨stick⟩ 7. ⟨click⟩ 8. ⟨back⟩
9. lake 10. ⟨quack⟩ 11. ⟨quick⟩ 12. ⟨sick⟩

Read each word group. Write the **ck** word from the word list that belongs with the group.

Word List: sock stick neck quick rock truck

13. fast, speedy, __quick__
14. log, twig, __stick__
15. shoulder, arm, __neck__
16. stone, pebble, __rock__
17. shoe, feet, __sock__
18. car, motorcycle, __truck__

135

Silent Letter in "mb"

Say the name of each picture. Fill in the circle next to the **mb** word that names the picture.

1. ● thumb / ○ dumb
2. ● climb / ○ tomb
3. ● lamb / ○ limb

Read each **mb** word. Write a sentence using the word. Circle the letters **mb**.

4. lamb
5. numb
6. crumb — Sentences will vary.
7. climb
8. comb

Area

Area is the space inside a figure. It is measured in **square units**. You can find the area by adding the number of squares in the figure.

Look at the following figures and find the area of each.

A. Area = __4__ square units
B. Area = __8__ square units

136

157

Answer Key

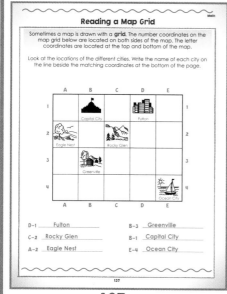

Reading a Map Grid

Sometimes a map is drawn with a **grid**. The number coordinates on the map grid below are located on both sides of the map. The letter coordinates are located at the top and bottom of the map.

Look at the locations of the different cities. Write the name of each city on the line beside the matching coordinates at the bottom of the page.

D–1 ___Fulton___ B–3 ___Greenville___
C–2 ___Rocky Glen___ B–1 ___Capital City___
A–2 ___Eagle Nest___ E–4 ___Ocean City___

137

Area and Perimeter

Rules:
Area **(A)** is the number of square units inside a figure. To find the area of rectangles and squares, multiply the length times the width.

Perimeter **(P)** is the number of units around a figure. To find the perimeter of rectangles and squares, add the length of all four sides.

Examples:
A = 4 x 3 = 12 square units
P = 4 + 3 + 4 + 3 = 14 units

A. Area = 9 square units Perimeter = 12 units
E. Area = 6 square units Perimeter = 10 units
B. Area = 10 square units Perimeter = 14 units
F. Area = 16 square units Perimeter = 16 units
C. Area = 20 square units Perimeter = 18 units
G. Area = 24 square units Perimeter = 20 units
D. Area = 18 square units Perimeter = 18 units
H. Area = 4 square units Perimeter = 8 units

138

Outcomes

An **outcome** is the result of an event.

Decide whether the following outcomes are **certain** (will definitely happen), **possible** (might happen), or **impossible** (will not happen). Write your answer on the line.

1. It will rain tomorrow. ___possible___
2. You will grow to be 50 feet tall. ___impossible___
3. The Vikings will win the Super Bowl next season. ___possible___
4. Tomorrow will be 24 hours long. ___certain___
5. Humans will travel to Mars. ___possible___
6. New Year's Eve will fall on December 31st. ___certain___

Homophones

Homophones are words that sound alike but are spelled differently and have different meanings.

Example: tall – tale

Circle the two words in each row that are homophones.

1. (bear) seen saw (bare)
2. violet vase (vain) (vein)
3. drop (dew) down (due)
4. (tee) tell told (tea)
5. well (weight) (wait) went
6. him (hair) (hare) held

139

Reading a Map

Marcia lives in Flower City. She has a new friend named Tina. Marcia invited Tina to her house for a visit. Marcia drew a map to help Tina find her house.

Look at the map and use it to answer the questions below.

1. The road where Marcia lives is ___Violet Road___
2. The lane where Tina lives is ___Daisy Lane___
3. What four roads cross the railroad tracks? ___Tulip Avenue, Daisy Lane, Zinnia Street, Daffodil Road___
4. What road intersects both Daffodil Road and Violet Road? ___Zinnia Street___
5. How can you get across Bubbling Creek? ___Take Tulip Avenue, Crocus Road, or Violet Road___
6. What roads intersect Zinnia Street? ___Daffodil Road, Violet Road___

140

Punctuation

Place the correct punctuation mark at the end of each sentence in the story below. Write an ending to the story.

Making Pancakes

My sister and I woke early last Saturday morning . We decided to make breakfast for Mom . We took out the pancake mix . We put the mix in a big bowl We added eggs and milk . I was stirring the batter . My sister was pouring orange juice . Then, the cat jumped onto the counter . He tipped over the glass of juice and knocked the bowl to the floor . Batter and juice went everywhere ! Next . . .

Endings will vary.

141

Understanding What I Read

Read the story. Then answer the questions.

Nightly Navigator

Many people do not realize what bats do for us. They are some of our best nighttime insect exterminators. Over 900 kinds of bats exist in the world today. These bats can be anywhere from one-half inch long to over 15 inches long. Although most bats eat just insects, some dine on fruit and the nectar of flowers. As the only flying mammals on earth, bats should be recognized for their contributions to humans. Aside from controlling the insect population, bats are the main pollinators and seed spreaders for many tropical trees like mangoes, guavas, cashews, cloves, and Brazil nuts. Bats use their sonar-guided mouths and ears to enjoy a nightly dinner of millions of mosquitoes, mayflies, and moths.

1. What is the main idea of this paragraph?
 ___Most people do not realize what bats do for us.___
2. How many different kinds of bats are there in the world?
 ___Over 900 kinds of bats exist in the world.___
3. What do bats like to eat?
 ___Bats eat insects, fruit, and the nectar of flowers.___
4. How large can some species of bats get?
 ___Bats can grow to over 15 inches long.___
5. What kinds of tropical trees depend on the bat for spreading their seeds and for pollination?
 ___Bats spread seed for mangoes, guavas, cashews, cloves, and Brazil nuts.___

142

How to Write a Friendly Letter

Review the five parts of a friendly letter.

July 10, 2002 — date
greeting — Dear Tim,
body — What a great time we had when you came to visit! I liked playing baseball and football with you. Swimming was fun, too. I hope that you will visit me again soon.
Your friend, — closing
Jason — signature

Write a letter to your friend. Talk about the things you like to do together.

(date)
(greeting)
Paragraphs will vary.
(closing)
(signature)

143

Write a Friendly Letter

Write a letter to a new friend. Be sure to include the five parts of a friendly letter.

Describe yourself.
Tell what you like to do.
Describe your room.
Describe your family.

Paragraphs will vary.

144

Addressing Envelopes

Address the envelopes below using the information given.

The sender is:
Dr. James Madison
38 Carlton Place
Salem, NC 29532

The receiver is:
Ms. Mary Morton
149 Sparrow Street
Tucson, AZ 52974

Dr. James Madison
38 Carlton Place
Salem, NC 29532

Ms. Mary Morton
149 Sparrow Street
Tucson AZ 52974

The sender is:
Mrs. Alice Watson
9 Flag Avenue
Port Huron, MI 48060

The receiver is:
Miss Susan Coats
183 Spring Street
Denver, CO 50738

Mrs. Alice Watson
9 Flag Avenue
Port Huron, MI 48060

Miss Susan Coats
183 Spring Street
Denver, CO 50738

145

Cut-and-Color Awards

Parent: Have your child decorate and color these awards. Fill in your child's name and the date to mark each accomplishment. The awards can be worn as badges or put into small frames.

I can arrange words and titles in alphabetical order!

Name: _____ Date: _____

I can add and subtract LARGE numbers!

Name: _____ Date: _____

I understand base words, prefixes, and suffixes!

Name: _____ Date: _____

I know my multiplication facts!

Name: _____ Date: _____

I know my division facts!

Name: _____ Date: _____

nouns verbs adverbs

I know my parts of speech!

adjectives

Name: _____ Date: _____

I can use punctuation correctly!

Name: _____ Date: _____

I know my vowel sounds and consonant blends and digraphs!

Name: _____ Date: _____